Vietta,

Thanks you very much for joining for Diversity.

Best wishes in all you do!

Dr. Ed

Intentional Diversity Transformation

Building An Inclusive Culture Using Transformational Analytics

Dr. Edward E. Hubbard, Ph.D.

Intentional Diversity Transformation: Building An Inclusive Culture Using Transformational Analytics

Copyright © 2021 by Dr. Edward E. Hubbard, Ph.D.

All rights reserved. The reproduction or utilization of this work in any form or by any electronic, mechanical or other means, known now or hereafter invented, including xerography, photocopying and recording and in any information storage and retrieval system, is forbidden without the prior written permission of Hubbard & Hubbard, Inc. and Dr. Edward E. Hubbard. This manual may not be changed or reprinted in any other form without prior written permission of the publisher. Printed in the United States of America.

ISBN 978-1-883733-33-9

GLOBAL INSIGHTS PUBLISHING

832 Garfield Drive, Petaluma, CA 94954
Office: (707) 481-2268   email:edhub@aol.com

Preface

Performance measurement in organizations is not something new, however, in the last 30 years or so, organizations have realized that financial measures alone are not sufficient for evaluating the success of an enterprise.

In the mid-1990s, the balanced scorecard concept was introduced; forcing executives to take a hard look at how many of their metrics were financial and then balance out their scorecards with nonfinancial metrics. The balanced scorecard approach also recommended that fewer metrics are better. The number of metrics that companies tracked had been increasing each year for many years, but Kaplan and Norton suggested that no one should have more than 15 to 20 metrics per scorecard. This is still a tough sell for analytical executives who love pouring over hundreds of charts and numbers each month.

The primary issue that Diversity must deal with is very hard for some to imagine and believe, that is, showing Diversity's measurable impact on organizational strategy and the financial bottom-line. The ability to utilize a diverse mix of human and other resources to create unique blend of strategy focused solutions, by its

Intentional Diversity Transformation

very nature, creates an innovative competitive process that is difficult to copy – thus making it a competitive advantage (largely invisible to competitors).

Although most organizations have come a long way in introducing better metrics for Diversity on their corporate scorecards, there is still a great deal of work to be done. Even the best scorecards need improvement in some key areas to evolve to the next level of performance impact. Metrics in several Diversity Scorecards focus on counting activities, not producing outcomes and organizational transformations. There is a distinct difference between generating "outputs" from scorecard action plans and producing "Strategic Outcomes" and "Intended Transformational Impacts". "Strategic Outcomes" and "Intended Transformational Impacts are defined as "the planned, intended measurable result or effect of an action, situation, or event; something that follows due to a planned execution of measurable actions which result in intended consequences (or unintended consequences) that add value and drive evidence-based change.

This book will help develop an Intentional Diversity Scorecard using Diversity Transformational Analytics® created by Dr. Edward E. Hubbard, Ph.D. to drive organizational change and "next level" impacts based upon a "Logic Model" framework. Diversity

Intentional Diversity Transformation

Transformational Analytics® is a registered trademark of Hubbard & Hubbard, Inc., All Rights Reserved.

How this Book is Organized

Part I presents a brief overview of the current status of Diversity Scorecards. Before moving to the next evolution in Diversity Scorecards, each chapter in Part I will provide an understanding of the need for Diversity measurement. It provides an informational and statistical business case for Diversity and Inclusion and addresses some critical measurement issues that will help you gain a solid foothold to establish Diversity's link to the organization's strategy.

Part II presents the Diversity Return on Investment (DROI®) model in a step-by-step process. At the conclusion, the reader has a clear understanding of the overall DROI® process. Examples are used to explain key element of the model and enhance application strategies used in an organization.

Part III provides the basic building blocks for assembling a DROI® based Intentional Diversity Transformation Scorecard using a "Logic Model" to report Diversity's contribution to the bottom-line.

Intentional Diversity Transformation

Each Intentional Diversity Transformation Scorecard dimension is explained and highlights critical measures and processes that clarify their use.

Part IV explains why the next generation of Diversity scorecards and their transformational metrics and analytics are superior to singular statistics. It will show you how to construct various types of Diversity Transformational Analytics® to improve your scorecard and Diversity business intelligence. It also contains an extended discussion on the use of "Predictive Evaluation" for Diversity and Inclusion Initiatives to drive forecasted results.

Intentional Diversity Transformation

Who Should Read this Book

This book is written for anyone who wants to analyze, measure, demonstrate, and/or improve his or her Diversity initiatives' impact and report results using a scorecard methodology, such as…

- Senior Executives and Managers
- Senior Vice Presidents of Diversity
- Chief Diversity Officers
- Diversity Council members
- Workforce Diversity Directors and Managers
- Global Diversity Executives
- Vice Presidents of Human Resources
- EEO and Affirmative Action Executives
- CEOs
- COOs
- Organization Development Specialists
- Etc.

This book is designed to help you learn how to implement an "intentional" Diversity scorecard measurement process to demonstrate Diversity's return-on-investment impact in the least amount of time. It will act as your coach and guide while providing implementation ideas to help carry out this process. It will also

Intentional Diversity Transformation

introduce you to the next level in Diversity metrics: Diversity Transformational Analytics®. Diversity Transformational Analytics® is a registered trademark of Hubbard & Hubbard, Inc., All Rights Reserved.

After working through the Diversity scorecard process outlined in this book, you will be able to:

- Build a Diversity Strategic Outcomes-based scorecard using a Logic Model framework.
- Link the "right" Diversity measures to the organization's measures of performance.
- Build a measurable business case for Diversity and Inclusion that is unique to your organization.
- Implement a multi-step process to evaluate Diversity's impact and contribution
- Identify some basic Diversity scorecard components.
- Construct a series of Hubbard Intentional Diversity Transformation Scorecard® indices that are link to the organization's key business drivers.
- Report results using your "enhanced" Intentional Diversity Transformation Scorecard metrics demonstrating their contribution and return-on-investment impact.

Intentional Diversity Transformation

- Plan how to track each Diversity and Inclusion measure in a "Logic-Chain" to produce an "intended outcome and impact that drives change".
- Address critical implementation issues that help integrate the "enhanced" Diversity scorecard into the fabric of the organization's normal mode of operating.

In addition, you will improve the accuracy and credibility of your Diversity metrics by linking them to critical success factors as well as learn how to select the right metrics which support organizational performance and success.

Acknowledgments

My first and deepest appreciation goes to my gifted, beautiful, caring wife, Dr. Myra Hubbard, Ph.D. You are truly my friend, soulmate and my rock. I continue the thank God every day for the blessings of you. You constantly give me inspiration and support to continue to do this work. Your suggestions and insights are always invaluable. I dedicate this book to you.

Secondly, I would like to thank my wonderful family. First, to my mother, Geneva Hubbard (in memoriam) whose love and strong foundation-setting values always keeps me strong. You left me with so many wonderful memories and guidelines to live by I will always treasure. Mom, the wisdom you gave us is my guiding light. To my sons, Chance and Ed II, I love you and I am so proud of you. To my Grandson, Jamil, whose blueprint for life is still under construction but developing rapidly. It is a joy to watch you grow and come into your own. I love your spirt of curiosity and persistence. What a precious gift from God. To my sisters Leona, Lois, Sylvia, Jan, Debbie, Sue, and their families, to Germaine, Harold, Frank and Janet, to my nieces and nephews, especially my nephew and niece Darrel and Rocki Branch, and niece Camille Haynes. You truly show your love and caring in so many ways. To Emilio Egea and

Intentional Diversity Transformation

Pastor Shane Wallis whom I can always count on to have my back when I need it most. Thank you for your authentic love and support. And to a host of other relatives and friends who always keep us in their prayers. Thank you for your love and caring.

The genesis of this book began almost 10 years ago when I reflected on one of my previous books – **"The Diversity Scorecard: Evaluating the Impact of Diversity on Organizational Performance"** and the current state of the fields of Diversity and Inclusion regarding measurement. I noticed the same ongoing need to have access to tools to more definitively drive Diversity change and transformation and the courage and discipline to use them. I am continually concerned that Diversity and Inclusion (D&I) Practitioners overall have not rigorously adopted and applied Diversity and Inclusion Sciences® to their daily work. This has led to D&I departments being viewed as less than a worthwhile investment compared to other departments. This practice has placed Diversity and Inclusion in the "line-of-sight" for reductions and/or elimination when times and budgets get tight. Even worse, D&I is not always viewed as a credible contributor to the bottom-line due to, in my opinion a lack of scientific application of well-founded organizational development, business process, and evidence-based, ROI-based metrics and analytics to prove its added value. Many in

Intentional Diversity Transformation

our discipline continue to use "Diversity representation" and "Inclusion" initiatives or interventions **without** evidence-based outcomes and impact as a means to show that Diversity and Inclusion progress is being made. It takes much more than that. It requires evidence which must be backed up by science and data that demonstrates real, tangible impact that has driven bottom-line financial and non-financial results. These efforts must credibly demonstrate the Diversity and Inclusion initiative's ability to drive the organization's achievement of goals, objectives, mission, and vision for success.

The goals and objectives of many Diversity departments is to create sustainable change for a culture of Inclusion where employees are valued and respected for who they are and to be seen as assets. From a measurement and analytics point of view, I have always been intrigued with developing a "systems and evidence-based" process that would drive intentional, sustainable change with predictive accuracy and feedback along the way. I have always felt that Diversity and Inclusion needed more scientific rigor and professional standards by which to operate in order to demonstrate its value and contribution with credibility (like other disciplines). After a great deal of personal research, application, reflection, and revision, I feel I found a "perfect storm" of sciences in Logic Models

Intentional Diversity Transformation

Development, ROI Measurement, Predictive Analytics, the utilization of advanced methodologies of "Organizational Development theory" as well as the fields of "Organizational Transformation" and Organizational Behavior" to address this challenge. I owe a debt of gratitude to all of the pioneers, scholars, and practitioners in these fields.

I am especially grateful to Dr. Jack Phillips and Dr. Patti P. Phillips for their seminal work in the ROI measurement field. Thank you always for your friendship, kindness, scholarly wisdom and insights. I am forever grateful for your contribution to the fields of evaluation and measurement. I would also like to thank my personal Diversity and Inclusion Mentors, the late Dr. R. Roosevelt Thomas, and the late Dr. Price Cobbs whose pioneering research is the foundation of the Diversity and Inclusion disciplines we know today. I stand on your shoulders to expand this work and build on their legacies. All of their scholarly research enhanced my work in continuing to create the **Hubbard Diversity and Inclusion Sciences®** to make a measurable difference in an organization's performance and the world's diverse cultural environments.

When writing any book, there are so many people whose gifts of sharing real-life stories and challenges help form the basis of your thoughts. I am forever grateful to all those individuals who allowed me to test and implement this model to prove its validity and whose words of encouragement and insights tweaked and adjusted my thoughts, based upon empirical evidence. Their support and the results convinced me that the **Hubbard Intentional Diversity Transformation Scorecard**® worked and was needed in my life-long quest to create *ROI-based sciences* for the fields of Diversity and Inclusion. Thank you all for making this book possible.

Dr. Edward E. Hubbard, Ph.D.

Hubbard & Hubbard, Inc.

International Organization and Human Performance Consulting Corporation

Performance – Metrics – ROI Impact

February, 2021

Table of Contents

Contents

Intentional Diversity Transformation 1

Building An Inclusive Culture Using Transformational Analytics 1

Intentional Diversity Transformation: Building An Inclusive Culture Using Transformational Analytics 2

Preface 3

How this Book is Organized 5

Who Should Read this Book 7

Acknowledgments 10

Table of Contents 15

Part I 23

The Need for Diversity Measurement 23

Chapter One: Beyond First and Second Generation Diversity Scorecards 25

Evolution of the Diversity "Balanced" Scorecard 26

Can a Perceived Intangible Asset Like Diversity Generate Tangible Benefits? 33

Problems with most Diversity Scorecards Today 39

Intentional Diversity Transformation

Problem: Scorecards Focus on Representation and Activity-based Metrics and Do Not Concentrate on Producing Outcomes and Organizational Transformations 41

Problem: Problems Still Exist in Aligning Goals, Strategies, and Metrics 43

Problem: Scorecards Are Not Deployed Beyond Senior Management Levels 44

Problem: Most Executive Bonuses Are Not Linked to Non-financial Metrics 45

Problem: Most Targets Are Still Set Arbitrarily 45

Problem: PowerPoint and Spreadsheets Are Still Being Use to Review Performance 46

Problem: Scorecards Never Include External Factors That Could Have a Huge Impact on an Organization's Success 48

Best Practice: Get Rid of Flawed Metrics 50

Best Practice: Measure Frequently 52

Summary 55

References 57

Chapter Two: The Business Case for Diversity 61

A Diversity Measurement Challenge: How Can We Ensure that Diversity Is "at" the Strategic Business Table, Not "on" the Menu?61

Can a Perceived Intangible Asset Like Diversity Generate Tangible Benefits? 66

Diversity Facts, Figures, and Financial Performance 71

What Do We Mean by Diversity? 73

Diversity Provides a Business Advantage 77

Intentional Diversity Transformation

Failure to Implement a Diversity Initiative Can Be Costly 83

Diversity Links to Productivity and Performance 86

Retention 87

Productivity 90

The Link Between the Lack of Diversity Programs and Absenteeism 93

Diversity's Contribution to the Bottom Line 96

Building Centers of Diversity Excellence 99

Final Thoughts 108

References 108

Chapter Three: Introduction to Diversity Measurement 113

It's All Subjective . . . or Is It? 113

Reasons for Lack of Quantification in Diversity 116

Challenges of Quantification 120

The Definition of Measurement 124

Outcome Measures or Performance Drivers? 132

Building a Solid Diversity Measurement Strategy 135

Final Thoughts 138

References 139

Part II 141

The Diversity Return on Investment (DROI®) Process and Transformational Analytics® 141

Chapter Four: Introduction to the Diversity ROI Process 143

Introduction 143

Intentional Diversity Transformation

What do we mean when we say "Diversity"? 143

What sites must be visited along the measurement journey? .. 145

Hubbard Diversity ROI Analysis Model 146

Analysis 146

Data Collection 147

Data Isolation 147

Data Conversion 147

Cost/Benefits Analysis 147

Tracking/Reporting 147

Analysis 147

Step 1: Know What You Want To Know 147

Data Collection 149

Step 2: Collect Data and Analyze It 149

Data Isolation 150

Step 3: Isolate Diversity's Contribution 150

Data Conversion 152

Step 4: Convert the Contribution to Money 152

Cost/Benefits Analysis 154

Step 5: Calculate the Costs and Benefits 154

Calculating the Diversity Initiative Costs 154

Calculating the Diversity Return on Investment 155

Identifying Intangible Benefits 156

Tracking/Reporting 157

Intentional Diversity Transformation

Step 6: Report It to Others 157

Step 7: Track and Assess Progress 158

Your Challenge 158

References 159

Chapter Five: Introduction to Diversity Transformational Analytics 161

Can Diversity & Inclusion Really Affect the Bottom-line with Predictive Transformational Impact? 161

What's Next? 162

Evolving the Diversity Scorecard's Business Impact 163

What are Analytics 163

Basic Logic Model 166

Logic Model to Build Strong Families 169

Logic Model for Program Development 171

Higher Education Focused Logic Model 174

Organizational Transformation and Change 183

Origins of Transformational and Transactional Dynamics 186

A Model of Organizational Performance and Change: 187

The TRANSFORMATIONAL Factors 187

A Model of Organizational Performance and Change: 190

The TRANSACTIONAL Factors 190

References 197

Chapter Six: The Transformational Diversity Scorecard 201

Intentional Diversity Transformation

An Innovative Evolution in Diversity ROI Metrics Design that Drives Strategic Evidence-based Results and Impact!................... 201

What Is a Balanced Scorecard? 202

The Balanced Scorecard as a Measurement System................ 203

When should the Hubbard Intentional Diversity Transformation Scorecard® be Used?.. 221

During planning to:.. 222

During implementation to:... 223

During staff and stakeholder orientation to: 223

During evaluation to: 223

During advocacy to:... 224

What are the benefits and limitations of the Hubbard Intentional Diversity Transformation Scorecard®?... 226

Limitations... 231

In Summary 233

References.. 235

Chapter Seven: Strategies to Implement and Track Transformational Diversity Scorecard Initiatives 237

Strategies for Implementing Your Hubbard Intentional Diversity Transformation Scorecard® 237

References.. 244

Chapter Eight: Predictive Analytics for Diversity (PAD^{tm}) - A Next Practice Approach 247

Introduction... 247

Benefits of Predictive Analytics for Diversity^{tm} 249

Intentional Diversity Transformation

Where to Start 250

The Predictive Analytics for Diversity™ Framework 253

Intention Evaluation 254

Belief Evaluation 259

Adoption Evaluation 261

Impact Evaluation 265

Predicting the Value of Diversity and Inclusion Initiatives 266

Diversity and Inclusion's Value and Worth 270

Why Predictive? 272

The Predictive Analytics for Diversity (PAD™) Sequence 273

References 276

Chapter Nine: Driving the Future of Diversity and Inclusion . 277

Other Resources 281

Diversity ROI Certification Institutes and Training 281

Hubbard Diversity ROI Institute 281

Earn Six Professional Certifications in Diversity ROI - Available ONLY from Hubbard & Hubbard, Inc. 282

Hubbard Diversity Measurement & Productivity Institute 285

Professional Competency-based Training and Skill-building . 285

Hubbard & Hubbard, Inc. Products and Services 286

Products Web 286

Hubbard ERG and BRG ROI Institute 286

Intentional Diversity Transformation

ERG and BRG Training, Skill-building, and ROI Measurement Techniques for Resource Group Leaders, Sponsors, and Members 286

Metriclink Dashboard and Scorecard Services 287

Comprehensive Online Performance Measurement and Management Services for Organizational Excellence 287

Performance Spotlights and Publishing Opportunities 288

Measuring ROI of Diversity Initiatives, ERG/BRG Initiatives, and Other Webinars 289

Index 291

Part I
The Need for Diversity Measurement

Chapter One: Beyond First and Second Generation Diversity Scorecards

Performance measurement in organizations is not something new, but in the last 30 years or so, organizations have realized that financial measures alone are not sufficient for evaluating the success of an enterprise.

In the mid-1990s, the balanced scorecard concept was introduced; forcing executives to take a hard look at how many of their metrics were financial and then balance out their scorecards with nonfinancial metrics. The balanced scorecard approach also recommended that fewer metrics are better. The number of metrics that companies tracked had been increasing each year for many years, but Kaplan and Norton suggested that no one should have more than 15 to 20 metrics per scorecard. This is still a tough sell for analytical executives who love poring over hundreds of charts each month.

Evolution of the Diversity "Balanced" Scorecard

Over the last 30 years or so, the approaches that organizations use to measure performance have gone through three clear phases or stages. Each phase has lasted 10 or 15 years, and with each successive phase, the practice of measuring performance has become more exact. The process still has a way to go to qualify as an exact science, but the measures are improving as well as the integrity of the data upon which these measures are based. Models like the Baldrige criteria have helped facilitate this systematic approach to measuring and managing performance.

After creating the fields of Diversity Measurement and Diversity ROI Analytics in 1997 with my book "Measuring Diversity Results", and soon followed with "How to Calculate Diversity Return on Investment" in 1999, I began reflecting on the need for a methodology to effectively organize Diversity and Inclusion metrics and analytics in a way to balance out the array of Diversity and Inclusion-based financial and non-financial metrics that drive a measureable difference in organizational performance. Kaplan and

Intentional Diversity Transformation

Norton's Balanced Scorecard approach provided the suitable building blocks to construct an organizing framework that aligned with a Diversity and Inclusion (D&I) strategy, if modified appropriately.

I realized that if you think of any particular field of study such as Marketing, Sales, Engineering, Medicine, they have both theory and science which undergirds their structure. Diversity and Inclusion had some wonderful people doing great work on the "theory" side such Dr. R. Roosevelt Thomas, Dr. Taylor Cox, Dr. Marilyn Loden, Dr. Judy Rosener, and others however, D&I did not have a well-defined science to measure it's impact. As a result, I began to create a series of measurement sciences and analytics for Diversity and Inclusion to provide a much needed dimension to the Diversity and Inclusion field. The scientific approaches I chose are rooted in the sciences of Mathematics, Organizational Behavior, Transformation and Change, Strategic Planning, Business Analysis, and others.

Many Diversity professionals and others interested in Diversity began to ask: "How will we be able to demonstrate diversity's contribution to the organization's bottom-line?" How do we show senior executives and others that Diversity is a strategic business partner that is aligned and linked to the strategic goals and objectives of the organization? How can we show compelling evidence of Diversity's measurable organizational performance impact and ability to improve work environment quality? How does the strategic Diversity process help your organization excel in the domestic and global marketplace and provide favorable returns to stockholders and stakeholders?

They found it challenging to effectively answer these questions. It is my experience that Diversity and Inclusion organizations have their own brand of strategy and visions and put forth a well-developed view (at least from their own perspective) regarding the strategic value of their efforts. However, senior leaders and line management were skeptical, at best, of Diversity's role in the organization's success and its ability to demonstrate financial and strategic contributions to the bottom-line. In many firms, executives and others wanted to believe the cliché that views "people as the organization's most important asset, however, they simply couldn't understand how Diversity realistically would make that vision a reality which results in a measurable difference in the organization's performance.

Intentional Diversity Transformation

Organizations typically define their Diversity efforts in terms of "race and gender" which get reflected in the elements it tracks on a regular basis. This list is usually sorted by demographic group and might include items such as number recruited, employee turnover, cost per hire, number of minority or women on the organization's Board of Directors, and employee attitudes. Now consider those Diversity attributes, which push beyond "race and gender", that you believe are crucial to the implementation of your organization's competitive strategy. In this list, you might include items such as penetrating diverse customer markets, reducing "cycle-time", capable and committed diverse work teams that generate new, paradigm-shifting ideas worth $300,000 or more in half the time of competitors, or metrics which help track and demonstrate improved "customer issue resolution processes", increased market share, shareholder value and the like.

How well does your existing Diversity measurement processes capture the "strategic Diversity drivers" that you identified in the second list? For most organizations there will not be a very close match between the two lists. Even more important, in those firms where Diversity professionals think there is a close match, frequently, the senior executives do not agree that this second list actually describes how Diversity creates value. In either case, there

Intentional Diversity Transformation

is a serious disconnect between what is measured, what is important to organizational performance.

These questions are fundamental because new economic realities are putting pressure on Diversity to widen its focus from the traditional role of guardian of ethnic representation, social justice, and well-being to a broader, more strategic role as an important strategic business partner. As a primary source of production and performance impact, our economy has shifted from physical to intellectual capital (which comes in all Diversity mixtures such as colors, backgrounds, genders, orientations, thinking styles, etc.). A good idea does not have a specific color, race, creed, gender, sexual orientation or physical ability. It's just a great ideas and it can come from anyone! As a result, senior Diversity managers are increasingly coming under fire to demonstrate exactly how they are helping the organization "organize, utilize, and support" this critically significant organizational asset to create improved performance and value.

The primary issue that Diversity must deal with is very hard for some to imagine and believe, that is, showing Diversity's measurable impact on organizational strategy and the financial bottom-line. The ability to utilize a diverse mix of human and other resources to create unique blend of strategy focused solutions, by its

Intentional Diversity Transformation

very nature, creates an innovative competitive process that is difficult to copy – thus making it a competitive advantage (largely invisible to competitors). At the **Hubbard Diversity Return on Investment Institute**, we have dedicated ourselves to creating Diversity and Inclusion Sciences® to credibly measure this impact.

For example, one of the scientific frameworks I created to explain how Diversity and Inclusion impacts the financial bottom-line of an organization is called the Hubbard Diversity Performance Drivers Model® (see an abbreviated version below).

Intentional Diversity Transformation

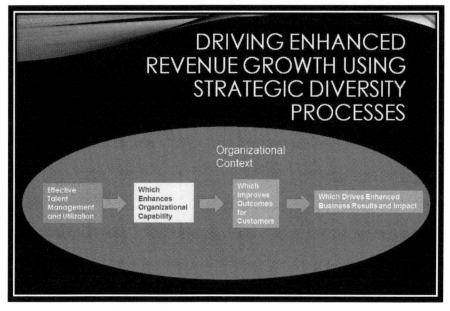

Source: "Hubbard Diversity Performance Drivers Model®" by Dr. Edward E. Hubbard, Ph.D. Copyright © 2008, All Rights Reserved. Proprietary Material

This model reflects that in order for Diversity to produce bottom-line results and impact, human capital assets (diverse talent) must be **"utilized"** to enhance organizational capability which if **"applied"** to key business challenges and issues can improve outcomes and results for customers which in turn drive increased or enhanced revenues that can be measured in ROI-value related terms. Representation alone does not generate improved revenue value. **Utilizing talent** from diverse backgrounds and mixtures that are applied to meet key strategic issues and challenges does.

Intentional Diversity Transformation

Simply put, "utilizing Diversity as a strategic asset" keeps an organization's competitive edge sharp for the long haul. This makes Diversity a prime source of sustainable competitive potential. However, to realize this potential, Diversity professionals must understand the organization's strategic plan for developing and sustaining this competitive advantage throughout the organization and its marketplace. If the organization is a non-profit, government, university, etc., then the organization's mission objectives must be fully understood and aligned with the Diversity and Inclusion strategy. In both cases, to gain Diversity's benefits, these human capital assets must be "utilized", not simply represented in the workforce.

Can a Perceived Intangible Asset Like Diversity Generate Tangible Benefits?

Yes, it can! Executives and other organizational personnel are beginning to recognize the importance and benefits of calculating the impact of perceived intangible human assets in today's marketplace. This has been challenging in the past for a number of reasons. As Becker, Huselid, and Ulrich (2001) pointed out, the accounting systems in use today evolved during a time when tangible capital, both financial and physical, constituted the principal source of profits. During this time, they state that the organizations which had the most access to money and equipment enjoyed a huge competitive advantage. With today's economic emphasis on knowledge and intangible assets, however, conventional accounting systems actually create dangerous informational distortions. As just one example, these systems encouraged limited, short-term thinking with respect to managing intangibles. Why? Because expenditures in these areas are treated as expenses rather than investments in assets. In contrast to this view, investments in buildings and machinery are capitalized and depreciated over their useful lives.

Consider the following dilemma faced by executives and managers: Decide whether to invest $10 million in hard assets or $10 million in people. In practical terms, when an organization invests $10 million in a building or physical asset, this investment is depreciated over time and earnings are reduced gradually over a 20- to 30-year period. In contrast, a $10 million investment in people is expensed in its entirety (and therefore earnings are reduced by $10 million) during the current year. For executives and managers whose pay is tied to this year's earnings (as many are), the choice of which investment to make is clear.

Intentional Diversity Transformation

As a result, organizations under financial pressure tend to invest in physical capital at the expense of human capital—even though the latter may very well generate more value. This kind of pressure can lead to poor decision-making behavior, such as using personnel layoffs, downsizing, and right-sizing to generate short-term cost savings. We know from past experience that after a layoff, the market may initially respond with a jump in share value; however, investors often eventually lose most, if not all, of these gains. This pattern is not surprising, given that people are a crucial source of competitive advantage rather than an expensive luxury that should be minimized.

The clear bottom line is this: If current accounting methods cannot give Diversity professionals the measurement tools they need, then it is imperative that we, as Diversity professionals, develop our own ways of demonstrating Diversity's contribution to the organization's performance. Like any other discipline, Diversity must be composed of both solid theory and applied sciences to gain credibility as a key contributor to organizational performance. At some point, the theory has to be put into practice and evaluated for its ability to add measurable value and understanding to real organizational issues.

Intentional Diversity Transformation

As mentioned previously, we had evidence of a great deal of solid "Diversity theory", such as those put forth by R. Roosevelt Thomas (1991,1996, 1999), Judith Rosner (1991), Marilyn Loden (1996), Taylor Cox (1993, 1997), and many others; however, notwithstanding the foundational Diversity measurement work completed by Edward E. Hubbard (1997, 1999), the Hubbard Diversity Measurement and Productivity Institute's research, and a chapter on the subject by Lawrence M. Baytos (1995), there had been little scientific inquiry research and operational processes which measured the real financial impact of Diversity.

The first step in building a Diversity contribution process required that we discard the accounting mentality that suggests Diversity or human resource–based efforts are primarily cost centers in which cost minimization is the primary objective and measure of success. At the same time, it was important to take advantage of the opportunity to help define the standards for measuring Diversity's impact. Investors and organizations such as the Swedish firm Skandia had made it clear that intangible assets are important. Skandia, for example, includes intellectual assets as a normal part of its profit and loss (P&L) reporting.

Intentional Diversity Transformation

My previous work pioneered efforts to create a wide variety of measures for the Diversity field in books such as *"Measuring Diversity Results"* (1997) and *"How to Calculate Diversity Return on Investment"* (1999) which copyrighted Diversity Return on Investment (DROI®) processes.

A few of the more than 55 books by Dr. Edward E. Hubbard, Ph.D.

Intentional Diversity Transformation

In addition to these books, I created the Hubbard Diversity Measurement and Productivity (HDM&P) Institute. The HDM&P Institute and Hubbard Diversity ROI Institute are dedicated to creating applied sciences, tools, strategies, frameworks, and processes for measuring the ROI impact of Diversity initiatives and their outcomes to improve organizational performance.

To focus exclusively on the development of Diversity Return on Investment (DROI®) methods, metrics and processes, I created the Diversity Return on Investment Institute.

Intentional Diversity Transformation

To truly reap the benefits of a Diversity Return on Investment (DROI®) approach, like other disciplines, it is up to Diversity professionals to maintain the discipline to effectively deploy the DROI® measurement and analytical sciences which create a measurable value for the organization. This will help position Diversity as a legitimate strategic business partner.

A key ingredient of any organization's success is its ability to strategically utilize human capital and leverage performance-based measurement feedback as a competitive advantage. To sustain success, maintain high productivity levels, retain talented employees, create new systems, and keep its diverse customer base, an organization must know its strengths and weaknesses in order to improve its overall performance. It is critical to have the Diversity-related tools and systems required to lead a measurement and ROI-enriched Diversity implementation strategy. These tools must channel the energies, abilities, and specific knowledge held by a diverse workforce throughout the organization toward achieving its long-term strategic goals and objectives.

Problems with most Diversity Scorecards Today

Although most organizations have come a long way in introducing better metrics for Diversity on their corporate scorecards, there is

Intentional Diversity Transformation

still a great deal of work to be done. Even the best scorecards need improvement in some areas. Here is just a just a few of the problems I've seen with current Diversity Scorecards:

- Most metrics focus on "representation" only and do not include outcome-based metrics and analytics
- Many metrics focus on counting activities, not producing outcomes and transformations.
- Most metrics are lagging indicators and not an effective mix of lead and lag indicators.
- Problems still exist in aligning goals, strategies, and metrics.
- Diversity scorecards are not effectively deployed and tracked beyond senior management levels.
- Most executive bonuses are not linked to Diversity and non-financial, intangible metrics
- Diversity targets are still set arbitrarily. They are not based on a credible "Business and Performance Needs Analysis" which is measured later for degree of change, impact and resolution the organization has experienced.
- Most Diversity metrics are not tightly linked to driving business outcomes. They focus on counting Diversity representation and the number of activities delivered.

Intentional Diversity Transformation

- PowerPoint and spreadsheets are still being used to review performance instead of robust Diversity dashboards that show "Diversity Transformational Analytics®" (Diversity Transformational Analytics® is a Copyrighted process of Hubbard & Hubbard, Inc., All Rights Reserved.)
- Diversity scorecards never include external factors that could have a huge impact on an organization's success.

Let's examine some of these problems in more detail:

Problem: Scorecards Focus on Representation and Activity-based Metrics and Do Not Concentrate on Producing Outcomes and Organizational Transformations

Metrics in several Diversity Scorecards focus on counting activities, not producing outcomes and organizational transformations. There is a distinct difference between generating "outputs" from scorecard action plans and producing "strategic outcomes". An "output" is defined as "the amount of something produced by a person. When Diversity metrics focus on "outputs" it often leads to examining activities and counting what was produced. These outputs may generate measures such as:

- # Employees Trained
- # Members in a ERG/BRG
- # Sessions Held

Intentional Diversity Transformation

- # Attended
- # Events Conducted
- Etc.

Activities and counts alone, although important, do not effectively lead to organizational transformations that drive performance improvement, efficiency, effectiveness and the like.

"Strategic Outcomes", on the other hand, can be defined as "the planned, intended measurable result or effect of an action, situation, or event; something that follows due to a planned result or intended consequence. Strategic Outcomes drive organizational transformations to create "next level" impacts such as:

- Increased Sales
- Decreased Costs
- Increased Retention
- Increased Satisfaction
- Improved Productivity
- Increased Employee Engagement
- Increased Diversity & Inclusion Competent Employees

These Strategic Outcomes produce "value" for the organization such as:

- Strategic Objectives Accomplished
- Mission Objectives Achieved
- Competitive Advantage Created
- Enhanced Brand Image

Intentional Diversity Transformation

- New Market Segments Created
- Extended/Expanded Product Lines
- A World-class Diversity Friendly Environment
- Great Place to Work
- High Performing Workplace

"Diversity Transformation Metrics and Analytics" help you focus on goals and ends rather than actions and means. They are designed to build "strategic capability" that allows you to specifically produce "change" or an intended outcome or result that drives organizational performance and value.

Problem: Problems Still Exist in Aligning Goals, Strategies, and Metrics

Too many organizations still have goals and strategies for which there are no metrics on the Diversity scorecard. For example, one organization had a goal to improve communication, yet it had no means of measuring whether communications had improved. Another had a goal of becoming a great place to work for employees, but it had no way to measure that on the scorecard, other than turnover.

Intentional Diversity Transformation

In yet another example, millions of dollars was being spent on Unconscious Bias programs training thousands of staff members worldwide without a thorough Business and Performance Needs Analysis to show that "unconscious bias" was the **cause** of the problem they were trying to fix! There was no clear tie to one of the Diversity scorecard metrics and analytics that would show the gap was closed and improvement was achieved and reflected in evidence-based outcome terms. Quite often, this leads to Diversity and Inclusion initiatives/programs/solutions being seen as an expense and a poor return on the organization's investment. Individuals may come away from these programs feeling better for a while, however, in the long run, the problems return and organizational success remain in jeopardy.

Problem: Scorecards Are Not Deployed Beyond Senior Management Levels

The majority of work that gets done in an organization is done by workers and supervisors, not senior leaders. Yet many organizations with excellent scorecards have failed to develop Diversity scorecards for departments, supervisors, and individual contributors. *All* levels of employees need to have a scorecard that tells them how they are performing on their job responsibilities and

Diversity-related issues. Sharing managers' scorecards with employees is not the same as having your own scorecard.

Problem: Most Executive Bonuses Are Not Linked to Non-financial Metrics

A number of big corporations I have worked with have good balance in their scorecards, but executive compensation is still linked to a handful of lagging financial measures, such as growth and profit.

Often, this causes leaders to ignore Diversity and non-financial metrics that are critically important. There are some forward-thinking companies like FedEx that are confident enough in their customer and people metrics to link them to bonuses, but these companies are in the minority.

Problem: Most Targets Are Still Set Arbitrarily

Establishing red, *yellow,* and green targets or ranges is as important as the metric itself. Unfortunately, many Diversity targets are still set without reference to competitor performance, industry averages, or benchmarks. They seem to center on Diversity activities and representation only and do not focus on driving key business-related outcomes.

In addition, establishing a target that is too high or too low will not drive the right decision making and actions. I still see a lot of arbitrary stretch targets, with no thought given to the resources needed to achieve those targets or how achievement of one target may cause a decline in performance on another company metric. Diversity scorecard targets appear to focus on "transactional metrics" instead of "transformational metrics and analytics". These differences make the critical differences in performance. I will discuss these essential differences in more detail later in the book.

Problem: PowerPoint and Spreadsheets Are Still Being Use to Review Performance

Most organizations still use PowerPoint presentations and prepare reports of performance using spreadsheets that are difficult to read and interpret. The dreaded monthly review meeting has not changed much, even in organizations that have adopted more balanced scorecards. Excellent Diversity Dashboard and Scorecard software exists that is not being used. Online services such as Hubbard & Hubbard, Inc.'s "Metriclink" Online Strategic Performance Impact

Intentional Diversity Transformation

Service with interactive business intelligence helps to simplify tracking, analyzing, and interpreting Diversity and Inclusion initiative outcomes. The system's analysis and tracking features are rooted in Hubbard "Diversity Transformational Analytics® sciences and Diversity Return on Investment (DROI®) approaches. These Diversity ROI-based algorithms are built into the Dashboard and automatically display ROI-based results.

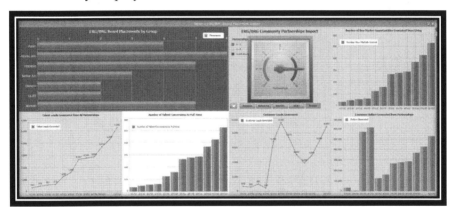

Source: Sample Hubbard Metriclink: ERG/BRG Board Placement Initiative Impact Dashboard and Scorecard. Copyright © 2010 by Hubbard & Hubbard, Inc. All Rights Reserved. Proprietary Material. Tel. 707-481-2268.

Intentional Diversity Transformation

Source: Sample Hubbard Metriclink: Higher Education Initiative Impact Dashboard and Scorecard. Copyright © 2010 by Hubbard & Hubbard, Inc. All Rights Reserved. Proprietary Material. Tel. 707-481-2268.

Problem: Scorecards Never Include External Factors That Could Have a Huge Impact on an Organization's Success

One of the big factors a pilot needs to monitor is weather. Although the pilot cannot do anything about the weather not having weather gauges in the cockpit would be unthinkable, a risk to safety and a huge mistake. The equivalent to weather gauges on an organization's scorecard might include factors such as the economy, the price of raw materials used by the firm, political trends, and business strategies of specific competitors, regulatory factors, brand image, and a number of other variables.

Intentional Diversity Transformation

A good balanced scorecard should include these external factors that are just as important as the company's own performance. Even though you can't control these factors any better than a pilot can control the weather, knowing they exist and what they imply for your organization can help you avoid turbulence. In spite of this, it is difficult to find a corporate or government scorecard that includes a weather gauge. Consequently, leaders are often making decisions and developing action plans based on how well the plane is operating, rather than on the conditions in which it is operating as well.

Diversity scorecards seem to suffer from the same malady. I have not seen Diversity scorecards that contain a suite of metrics and analytics that correlate with the business outcomes which they should be designed to drive such as revenue, innovation, market share, customer intimacy, brand and satisfaction. Although there are more dubious scorecard metrics and approaches than good ones, there are some best practices that deserve mention here. Some of the best practices simply do the opposite of the things listed above. Other best practices are described below:

Intentional Diversity Transformation

Best Practice: Get Rid of Flawed Metrics

This is probably the most prevalent problem with scorecards. Organizations put old Diversity metrics on their new Diversity scorecards even though everyone knows that performance on the measures can be easily manipulated. This happens in several different organizations that wanted to have a measure of project schedule and initiative performance on their new balanced scorecards. The concept behind the metric is solid: It measured percent milestones completed on major projects. Past performance on this measure showed it was always green throughout the course of a given project, yet customers and other stakeholders who depended on the project or initiative's results complained that the project failed to meet major initiative and project deadlines.

The problem with this measure was that the scheduled dates were always changed or adjusted when project managers saw that they were going to be missed. It was easy to justify the new deadlines because of changes to project scope or delays from suppliers/vendors. Throughout the course of a project, the schedule gauge looked green until the very end, when it turned red because the end date was missed. The main problem with this measure was that the schedule data lacked integrity-it was too easy for project managers to adjust the milestone dates to give the appearance that they were on schedule.

Intentional Diversity Transformation

An organization that builds and maintains ships for the U.S. Navy came up with a better approach. It measured the amount of "churn" or change there is to a project's scope, schedule, and budget. Some amount of churn is expected and acceptable, but too much indicated either a poor project plan, or a poorly managed project. Churn was easy to track because the data came right from the project management software that everyone used to monitor project progress.

This type of approach is also needed for managing a schedule of Diversity initiatives. Additionally, Diversity and Inclusion professionals need to learn to use key performance tracking tools such as project management software, Hubbard Online Metriclink Service for Diversity, and its reporting capabilities.

When people are allowed to select their own performance metrics, there is a tendency for them to pick measures that make them look good or can be easily manipulated. An objective outside facilitator such as a consultant can help minimize this self-serving approach, but it is often easy to snow the consultant or convince him or her that the proposed measures are valid. By the same token, internal facilitators often get overruled by senior managers. What ends up happening is that the new scorecard is no better than the old one.

Intentional Diversity Transformation

People go to meetings each month and look at the red, yellow, and green charts, but everyone knows that actual performance is often much different from what is depicted in the reports. A solution to this common phenomenon is to use a separate group of inside or outside experts to review proposed metrics to look for data integrity problems. You might take your draft scorecard to several outside experts and ask them to spend a day or so reviewing the metrics and provide feedback. It is also a good idea to have some of your own people do this. Incorporating reviews like this can go a long way toward weeding out the bad metrics.

Best Practice: Measure Frequently

There is no business in the world that would think of measuring financial performance once a year. Instead, most managers and entrepreneurs measure financial and operational performance *daily*. The more often you measure something, the better you can manage it. For example, diabetics monitor their blood sugar several times a day; some people monitor their blood pressure every day. Fortunately, most business and government organizations seem to agree with this concept and have no problem with the cost and time it takes to monitor financial and operational performance on a daily and weekly basis.

Intentional Diversity Transformation

On the other hand, if you look at these same organizations and ask them how often they measure customer satisfaction, employee satisfaction, and other "softer," but no less important aspects of their performance, they usually say, "Once a year." In fact, one company we worked with measured employee satisfaction every *other year*. When the score went down, company executives began busily working on many initiatives to improve morale. When asked how things were going, they replied, "We don't know, we need to wait another 20 months to get another data point." With such a lengthy time frame, this organization will end up wasting a lot of money and time working on initiatives that do absolutely nothing to improve employee satisfaction.

The take-home message here is that if something is important enough to measure at all, you need to measure it frequently. Annual metrics are close to worthless, and they function more like a historical study rather than as a performance measure. Of course, the more frequently you measure something, the more it usually costs. The challenge is to come up with a way to measure performance often without spending a lot of money. This is both practical and feasible.

One client, for example, used to spend $100,000 a year to have some university conduct an annual survey of employee satisfaction. *A* team came up with the idea of measuring morale on a daily basis by

Intentional Diversity Transformation

giving all employees a bag of red, yellow, and green marbles. At the end of the day, employees now drop a marble in a vase by the door where they usually leave, depending on how good or bad of a day they had (red = a really bad day, yellow = a fair day, and green = a really good day). Each morning, the boss's assistant counts up the marbles by department, and managers talk to their people if there are a lot of red and yellow marbles from the previous day. The entire system costs less than $1000 per year to implement, provides a daily statistic on morale by department, and forces managers to talk to their people on a daily basis about working conditions and other issues.

Another client used to spend more than $100,000 each year for an annual customer survey that was used to produce a big report and a once-a-year data point. Using a diverse team, this company also discovered that customer satisfaction data did not correlate to customer loyalty. To correct the discrepancy, it came up with a "Customer Aggravation Index" that it could track on a daily basis. The index measured operational and quality problems that were already being tracked, things that tend to make customers angry, such as being put on hold when calling the call center, late deliveries, errors on invoices, etc. The company found a direct correlation between levels of customer aggravation and loyalty. In other words, the measure confirmed that screwing up and making customers angry resulted in customers taking their business elsewhere-usually without bothering to fill out a survey. This metric involved little investment to implement because most of the aggravations were already being tracked.

Summary

There are a number of dimensions that characterize a good scorecard:

- There *are* more predictive metrics and fewer lagging ones.
- There are very few singular metrics on executives' scorecards.
- Metrics are better aligned with goals, strategies, and plans.
- All Diversity improvement initiatives are linked to one or more business scorecard metrics tied to business goals and objectives.
- Diversity Scorecards are not just for leaders and managers; all levels of employees need scorecards.
- Scorecard data are presented electronically online with few PowerPoint charts and without spreadsheets.
- Metrics on the scorecard are the real numbers used to run the Diversity and Inclusion organization's initiatives that are tied to the business.

Intentional Diversity Transformation

- High-level metrics are *made* of a number of layers of sub-metrics.
- Hubbard Diversity Business Alignment Maps (D-BAMs®) and Hubbard Diversity sciences are used to develop processes and leading indicators.
- Performance review meetings involve looking at live real-time data, not prepared charts of history alone.

Performance measurement and management have clearly taken hold in the Diversity and Inclusion fields. Most forward-thinking business and government organizations have implemented a measurement structure that includes more than the traditional lagging measures of financial and operational performance. Nevertheless, many scorecard projects fail because of either poor design or poor implementation. In contrast, successful projects are characterized by an approach that:

- Eliminates old flawed metrics and replaces them with ones with good integrity;
- Includes metrics that can be tracked frequently (e.g., quarterly or monthly);
- Is a simple scorecard architecture that will actually be implemented; and
- Focuses on actual tracking of the new metrics rather than continually redrawing the scorecard to try to make it perfect.

Intentional Diversity Transformation

Diversity scorecards must evolve too to remain effective. They must move well-beyond representation-based, transaction metrics to take advantage of more effective and impactful transformation-focused metrics and analytics.

References

Addison Reid, Barbara. "Mentorships Ensure Equal Opportunity." *Personnel Journal*, November 1994, 122–123.

Baytos, Lawrence M. *Designing & Implementing Successful Diversity Programs*. Englewood Cliffs, NJ: Prentice Hall, 1995.

Becker, Brian E., Mark A. Huselid, and Dave Ulrich. *The HR Scorecard: Linking People, Strategy, and Performance*. Boston: Harvard Business School Press, 2001.

Capowski, Genevieve. "Managing Diversity." *Management Review*, 85: 13–19.

Cox, Taylor Jr. *Cultural Diversity in Organizations*. San Francisco: Berrett-Koehler, 1993.

Cox, Taylor, Jr., and Ruby L Beale. *Developing Competency to Manage Diversity*. San Francisco: Berrett-Koehler, 1997.

Davis, Drew. "Beyond Casual Fridays: Are Managers Tuned in to Workplace Culture?" *Canadian HR Reporter*, May 6, 1996, 17.

Haskett, James L., Thomas O. Jones, Gary W. Loveman, Earl W. Sasser, Jr., and Leonard A Schlesinger. "Putting the Service-Profit Chain to Work." *Harvard Business Review*, March/April 1994, 164–174.

Haskett, James L., Earl W. Sasser, Jr., and Leonard A. Schlesinger. *The Service Profit Chain*. New York: The Free Press, 1997.

Hubbard, Edward E. *How to Calculate Diversity Return on Investment*. Petaluma, CA: Global Insights, 1999.

Hubbard, Edward E. *Measuring Diversity Results*. Petaluma, CA: Global Insights, 1997.

IBM and Towers Perrin. *Priorities for Competitive Advantage*. New York: IBM and Towers Perrin, 1991.

Kaplan, Robert S., and David P. Norton. *The Balanced Scorecard*. Boston: Harvard Business School Press, 1996.

Lapp, Janet. *Plant Your Feet Firmly in Mid-Air*. Albany, NY: Delmar, 1996.

Loden, Marilyn. *Implementing Diversity*. Chicago: Irwin, 1996.

Loden, Marilyn, and Judith Rosener. *Workforce America*. Homewood, IL: Business One Irwin, 1991.

Martinez, Michelle Neely. "Equality Effort: Sharpens Bank's Edge." *HR Magazine*, January 1995, 38–43.

Poole, Phebe-Jane. *Diversity: A Business Advantage*. Ajax, Ontario: Poole Publishing, 1997.

Reichheld, Frederick F., and Earl W. Sasser, Jr. "Zero Defections: Quality Comes to Services." *Harvard Business Review*, October 1990.

Rucci, Anthony J., Steven P. Kirn, and Richard T. Quinn. "The Employee-Customer-Profit Chain at Sears." *Harvard Business Review*, 76(1):1998, 90.

Thomas, R. Roosevelt, Jr. *Beyond Race and Gender*. New York: AMACOM, 1991.

Thomas, R. Roosevelt, Jr. *Building a House for Diversity*. New York: AMACOM, 1999.

Thomas, R. Roosevelt, Jr. *Redefining Diversity*. New York: AMACOM, 1996.

See "No More Business as Usual," *Working Woman*, Special Advertising Section: Strength Through Diversity for Bottom-line Success: A Call

Intentional Diversity Transformation

to Manage Diversity. MacDonald Communications Corporation, March 1999.

Von Eron, Ann M. "Ways to Assess Diversity Success." *HR Magazine*, August 1995, 51–60.

Wenger, Etienne, Richard McDermott, and William M. Snyder. *Cultivating Communities of Practice*. Boston: Harvard Business School Press, 2002.

Chapter Two: The Business Case for Diversity

A Diversity Measurement Challenge: How Can We Ensure that Diversity Is "at" the Strategic Business Table, Not "on" the Menu?

Many Diversity professionals and others interested in Diversity have asked the following questions:

- How will we be able to demonstrate that Diversity contributes to the organization's bottom line?
- How do we show senior executives and others that Diversity is a strategic business partner that is aligned and linked to the strategic goals and objectives of the organization?
- How can we measure the impact of Diversity on organizational performance and an improved work environment?

- How does the strategic Diversity process help an organization excel in the domestic and global marketplace and provide favorable returns to stockholders and stakeholders?

If your organization is like most, you have probably found it challenging to answer these questions. Experience has shown that the Diversity organization has its own brand of strategy and visions and has developed its own perspective regarding the value of its efforts to implement a diverse work environment; however, senior leaders and line management are skeptical, at best, of diversity's impact on the organization's success and their ability to demonstrate any financial or strategic contributions that a diverse workforce makes to the bottom line. In many firms, executives and others want to believe the cliché that views people as the organization's most important asset; however, they simply cannot understand how diversity realistically makes that vision a reality that results in a measurable difference in organizational performance.

Intentional Diversity Transformation

Organizations typically define their Diversity efforts in terms of race and gender, which get reflected in the elements they track regularly. This list is usually sorted by demographic group and might include items such as number recruited, employee turnover, cost per hire, number of minority personnel or women on the organization's board of directors, and employee attitudes. Now consider those diversity attributes that push beyond race and gender that you believe are crucial to implementing your organization's competitive strategy. In this list, you might include items such as penetrating diverse customer markets, retaining capable and committed diverse work teams that generate new, paradigm-shifting ideas in half the time of competitors, new patents that are generated through diverse teams working on innovative approaches, improving customer issue resolution processes, reducing cycle time, increasing market share and shareholder value, and the like.

How well do your existing processes illustrate the strategies you use to help drive the accomplishment of the organization's business objectives? How well do your existing diversity measures capture the strategic Diversity drivers you identified in the second list? For most organizations, there will not be a very close match between the two lists. Even more important, in those firms where diversity professionals think there is a close match, the senior executives

Intentional Diversity Transformation

frequently do not agree that this second list actually describes how Diversity creates value. In either case, a serious disconnect exists between what is measured and what is important to organizational performance. This highlights why constructing a Diversity Business Alignment Map (D-BAM) is essential to illustrate the connection to the organization's Vision, Mission, Values, and key business outcomes (see Sample Hubbard D-BAM with Diversity Strategy below).

Sample Hubbard D-BAM with Diversity Strategy

Mission Level	Be the leading biotechnology company, using genetic information to discover, develop, commercialize and manufacture biotherapeutics that address significant unmet medical needs. (Oncology, Immunology, Angiogenics)				
Values Level	Superior Products and Customer Focus	Profitable Growth	Delegation and Accountability	Diversity	Trust and Respect
	Scientific Leadership	Exceptional People	Teamwork and Collaboration	Open, Direct Communication	Informal, Enjoyable Environment
Key Drivers Level	Aggressive Product Pipeline	Innovative Science	Commercial Powerhouse and Market Maker	High Standards of Performance & Productivity	Patient Empowerment & Customer Satisfaction	Alliances, Partnerships & Collaboration
	Aggressive Talent Pipeline	Scientific and Operational Excellence	Develop Future Leaders		Great Place to Work	Solid Ethics and Integrity
Strategic Diversity Level	Recruit for Existing and Emerging Needs		Develop Full Potential and Capabilities for All Employees		Include A Diverse Perspective for creative innovation in all business
	Strategic Outreach Sources	Diversity / Staffing/DNA Group Collaborations	Diversity Curriculum Road Map	Development & Succession Planning	Multi-Ethnic Healthcare and Emerging Markets	DNA/DC Group Guidance Bans
	AAP Planning	GNE Scholars Program	Managing Inclusion Follow-up	Functional DNA Plans	Business Partner & Supplier Program	Community Educational Initiatives
	Applicant Flow & ROI	Demographic Analysis	PP&R Diversity Capability	Inclusive Leadership Strategies	Climate Analysis Strategy	Diversity Networking Events

These questions are fundamental because new economic realities are putting pressure on organizations to widen their traditional focus of Diversity as the guardian of ethnic representation and social well-being to a broader, more strategic factor in business success. As a primary source of production and performance impact, our economy has shifted from physical to intellectual capital (which comes in all colors, backgrounds, genders, orientations, thinking styles, and so on). As a result, senior Diversity managers are increasingly coming under fire to demonstrate exactly how they are helping the organization organize, utilize, and document this critically significant organizational asset to create performance and value.

The primary issue that Diversity must deal with is difficult for some to imagine and believe (i.e., showing diversity's measurable impact on organizational strategy and the financial bottom line). The ability to utilize a diverse mixture of human and other resources to create a unique blend of strategy-focused solutions, by its very nature, creates an innovative competitive process that is difficult to copy—thus making it a competitive advantage (largely invisible to competitors).

Intentional Diversity Transformation

As mentioned previously, simply put, utilizing Diversity as a strategic asset keeps an organization's competitive edge sharp for the long haul. This makes Diversity a prime source of sustainable competitive potential. To realize this potential, however, diversity professionals must understand the organization's strategic plan for developing and sustaining this competitive advantage throughout the organization and its marketplace. In order to gain its benefits, this Diversity must be utilized.

Can a Perceived Intangible Asset Like Diversity Generate Tangible Benefits?

Yes, it can! Executives and other organizational personnel are beginning to recognize the importance and benefits of calculating the impact of perceived intangible human assets in today's marketplace. This has been challenging in the past for a number of reasons. As Becker, Huselid, and Ulrich (2001) point out, the accounting systems in use today evolved during a time when tangible capital, both financial and physical, constituted the principal source of profits. During this time, they state, those organizations that had the most access to money and equipment enjoyed a huge competitive advantage. With today's economic emphasis on knowledge and intangible assets, however,

Intentional Diversity Transformation

conventional accounting systems actually create dangerous informational distortions. As just one example, these systems encourage limited, short-term thinking with respect to managing intangibles. Why? Because expenditures in these areas are **treated as expenses rather than investments** in assets. In contrast to this view, investments in buildings and machinery are capitalized and depreciated over their useful lives.

Consider the following dilemma faced by executives and managers: Decide whether to invest $10 million in hard assets or $10 million in people. In practical terms, when an organization invests $10 million in a building or physical asset, this investment is depreciated over time and earnings are reduced gradually over a 20- to 30-year period. In contrast, a $10 million investment in people is expensed in its entirety (and therefore earnings are reduced by $10 million) during the current year. For executives and managers whose pay is tied to this year's earnings (as many are), the choice of which investment to make is clear.

As a result, organizations under financial pressure tend to invest in physical capital at the expense of human capital—even though the latter may very well generate more value. This kind of pressure can lead to poor decision-making behavior, such as using personnel layoffs, downsizing, and right-sizing to generate short-term cost savings. We know from past experience that after a layoff, the market may initially respond with a jump in share value; however, investors often eventually lose most, if not all, of these gains. This pattern is not surprising, given that people are a crucial source of competitive advantage rather than an expensive luxury that should be minimized.

The clear bottom line is this: If current accounting methods cannot give Diversity professionals the measurement tools they need, then it is imperative that we, as Diversity professionals, develop our own ways of demonstrating Diversity's contribution to the organization's performance. Like any other discipline, Diversity must be composed of both solid theory and applied sciences to gain credibility as a key contributor to organizational performance. At some point, the theory has to be put into practice and evaluated for its ability to add measurable value and understanding to real organizational issues.

We have evidence of a great deal of solid Diversity theory, such as those put forth by R. Roosevelt Thomas (1991, 1996, 1999), Judith Rosner (1991), Marilyn Loden (1996), Taylor Cox (1993, 1997), and many others; however, notwithstanding the seminal Diversity measurement work completed by Edward E. Hubbard (1997, 1999),

Intentional Diversity Transformation

2004, 20010, et.al., the Hubbard Diversity Measurement and Productivity Institute's research, and a chapter on the subject by Lawrence M. Baytos (1995), there has been little scientific inquiry research and operational processes that measure the real financial impact of Diversity.

The first step in building a diversity contribution process is to discard the accounting mentality that suggests diversity or human resource–based efforts are primarily cost centers in which cost minimization is the primary objective and measure of success. At the same time, it is important to take advantage of the opportunity to help define the standards for measuring diversity's impact. Investors and organizations such as the Swedish firm Skandia have made it clear that intangible assets are important. Skandia, for example, includes intellectual assets as a normal part of its profit and loss (P&L) reporting.

Dr. Edward E. Hubbard pioneered efforts to create a wide variety of measures for the Diversity field in his books *Measuring Diversity Results* (1997), *How to Calculate Diversity Return on Investment* (1999), *The Diversity Scorecard: Evaluating the Impact of Diversity on Organizational Performance* (2004), *Implementing Diversity Measurement and Diversity Management* (2004), *Diversity*

Intentional Diversity Transformation

Training ROI (2010), *Measuring the ROI Impact of ERGs and BRGs* (2014), *Diversity Return On Investment (DROI) Fundamentals* (2014), and many more. He has written over 40 Diversity Measurement and Business-related books and hundreds of articles on the subject. In addition to these books, Dr. Hubbard founded the Hubbard Diversity Measurement and Productivity (HDM&P) Institute. The HDM&P Institute is dedicated to creating applied sciences for measuring diversity performance and results to improve organizational performance. It is really up to diversity professionals to develop a new measurement system that creates real value for the organization. This will help position the Diversity and Inclusion organization as a legitimate strategic business partner.

A key ingredient of any organization's success is its ability to strategically utilize human capital and leverage performance-based measurement feedback as a competitive advantage. To sustain success, maintain high productivity levels, retain talented employees, create new systems, and keep its diverse customer base, an organization must know its strengths and weaknesses in order to improve its overall performance. It is critical to have the diversity tools and systems required to lead a measurement-managed diversity implementation strategy. These tools must channel the energies, abilities, and specific knowledge held by a diverse

Intentional Diversity Transformation

workforce throughout the organization toward achieving its long-term strategic goals and objectives.

Diversity Facts, Figures, and Financial Performance

Diversity professionals are increasingly challenged to take a more strategic perspective regarding their role in producing results for the organization. As Diversity professionals respond to these challenges, measuring the impact of Diversity and its contribution to the organization's performance will consistently emerge as a critical theme. This should really come as no surprise because over the last 5 to 7 years there has been an ever-increasing appreciation for the value of the softer people side or intangible assets of the organization's business and an associated trend toward strategic performance measurement systems, such as those of Robert Kaplan and David Norton's *The Balanced Scorecard* (1996). The Hubbard Diversity Business Alignment Map (D-BAM) (Hubbard, 2017) process provides a strategic, systemic approach to operationalize the Diversity strategy as an "integrated" methodology to reap the benefits of utilizing Diversity and Inclusion as a measurable performance improvement technology. This approach provides a strategy to address business challenges head on.

Intentional Diversity Transformation

During the past few years, several surveys of executives and human resource professionals have identified broad areas of Diversity as one of the top priorities now and in the immediate future. Certainly, the growth of consulting firms, seminars, conferences, and publications are evidence of the interest and needs of organizations. The staying power of Diversity as a corporate priority has been demonstrated by the high level of interest that carried through even the recession periods of the 90s and the beginning of the 21st century. In fact, in our past during the early part of the 90s, Towers Perrin reported in a survey that 96 percent of the responding companies had either maintained or increased their support for Diversity management during the recession. The HDM&P Institute conducted a Diversity measurement benchmarking survey in 2001 that reflected similar results. This survey found that 83 percent of the responding organizations planned to spend either the same amount or more on Diversity in 2002. Studies by organizations such as the Association for Talent Development (ATD – formerly ASTD) and i4cp) highlight the continued interest in Diversity. Yet at the same time, current studies indicate that the C-Suite has requested Diversity and Inclusion demonstrate measurable returns on the organization's investments in these areas and are sadly disappointed with the reporting on these efforts and the results. The D-BAM Methodology and model overcomes these weaknesses and helps deliver real measurable value to C-Suite to meet Stakeholder requirements. The business case for Diversity is compelling and must be addressed using critical business acumen and scientific processes to level-set Diversity and Inclusion as a strategic business partner like other areas of the business.

What Do We Mean by Diversity?

To begin, what do we mean by the term "***Diversity***"? According to Dr. R. Roosevelt Thomas, "*Diversity* can be defined as a collective mixture characterized by differences and similarities that are applied in pursuit of organizational objectives" (Thomas, 1996, 1999). *Diversity management* is "the process of planning for, organizing, directing, and supporting these collective mixtures in a way that adds a measurable difference to organizational performance." (Hubbard, 1999)

According to Dr. Hubbard, Diversity Management can be organized into four interdependent and sometimes overlapping aspects: Workforce Diversity, Behavioral Diversity, Structural Diversity, and Business and Global Diversity (Hubbard, 1999).

Intentional Diversity Transformation

Workforce Diversity encompasses group and situational identities of the organization's employees (i.e., gender, race, ethnicity, religion, sexual orientation, physical ability, age, family status, economic background and status, and geographical background and status). It also includes changes in the labor market demographics.

Behavioral Diversity encompasses work styles, thinking styles, learning styles, communication styles, aspirations, beliefs/value system, as well as changes in employees' attitudes and expectations.

Structural Diversity encompasses interactions across functions, across organizational levels in the hierarchy, across divisions and between parent companies and subsidiaries, and across organizations engaged in strategic alliances and cooperative ventures. As organizations attempt to become more flexible, less layered, more team-based, and more multi- and cross-functional, measuring this type of diversity will require more attention.

Business and Global Diversity encompasses the expansion and segmentation of customer markets, the diversification of products and services offered, and the variety of operating environments in which organizations work and compete (i.e., legal and regulatory context, labor market realities, community and societal expectations/relationships, business cultures and norms). Increasing

Intentional Diversity Transformation

competitive pressures, globalization, rapid advances in product technologies, changing demographics in the customer bases both within domestic markets and across borders, and shifts in business/government relationships all signal a need to measure an organization's response and impact on business Diversity.

Lawrence Bayos (1995) suggested that the 3 Ds have generated widespread corporate concern and interest in addressing diversity management issues, whether an organization has 100 or 100,000 employees. The 3 Ds are as follows:

Demographics. Females, minorities, and foreign-born personnel are projected to produce 85 percent of the net new growth in the U.S. workforce, while white males are fast becoming a minority in the workforce. In 1960, nine out of ten consumers were white. Currently, it is estimated that only six out of ten are white. The changing demographics of the workplace are also the changing demographics of the marketplace. Organizations are looking at ways to align their organizations to the new realities of their customer bases.

Disappointment. The traditional U.S. method for handling diversity was to bring women and people of color into the workforce under the banner of affirmative action. In doing so, it is often

Intentional Diversity Transformation

assumed that those individuals possess some deficiencies and may not have been hired if not for affirmative action. It was also assumed that they should be willing to assimilate their differences to better fit the norms of the majority group (usually white males) and thereby enhance their opportunities for recognition and advancement. In other words, to "make it," females and people of color would have to leave their needs and differences at the organization's front door. After a little more than three decades of affirmative action, it seems clear that the existing model has resulted in females and people of color being trapped in lower levels of the organizational pyramid. Turnover, discontent, and underutilization of talent are by-products of using the previous approaches for several decades.

Demands. The demands for new approaches to Diversity come from employees who have become less willing than their predecessors to assimilate their points of difference in hopes of gaining the elusive acceptance into the club. Furthermore, the intense pressure of industry and global competition to reengineer the organization requires that organizations tap the full potential of all their human assets.

Intentional Diversity Transformation

Diversity Provides a Business Advantage

Organizations that want to thrive in today's global marketplace know that they have to focus well beyond adding technology, efficient production processes, and innovative products. In fact, it can be argued that none of these approaches will add significantly measurable improvements unless all employees have an environment that allows them to do their absolute personal best work using their full capability. Forward-thinking organizations know that their competitive strength lies in focusing on their employees and their clients. For an organization to improve performance and results, it must be able to attract, motivate, and retain high-potential employees—including men and women from all backgrounds and walks of life.

In addition to attracting and retaining the best workforce, successful businesses must also attract and retain clients. The ability to retain clients can have a major impact on the organization's bottom line. For example, the lifetime revenue stream from a loyal pizza eater can be $12,000, a Cadillac owner $332,000, and a corporate purchaser of commercial aircraft literally billions of dollars (Haskett et al., 1994). A White House Office of Consumer Affairs study estimates that 90 percent of unhappy customers will not tell you they are unhappy with your service. Only 10 percent will complain. They also estimate that each unhappy person will tell nine other people

Intentional Diversity Transformation

about your poor service. They in turn will tell nine others. Therefore, 81 people will learn about your poor service.

If your business is a local coffee shop and 100 diverse customers (who order a $3 Café Mocha each week) were unhappy with your service, these potential $3–per-week coffee-drinking customers can potentially affect the success of your business in a major way, which may not be completely obvious until it is too late. For example, if these 100 unhappy customers tell nine others, 900 people will know about your poor service. If they choose not to come to your coffee shop for one day per week, then you have just potentially lost $1,263,600 in one year from only 100 customers!

Globalization and changing domestic markets reflect a changing buying public. It is no longer homogeneous. There is little doubt that an organization that is serious about diversity can gain an improved understanding of diverse customers' needs and therefore foster better customer service to an increasingly diverse market.

Some of the latest American workforce projections put forth by the U.S. Department of Labor indicate that only 15 percent of the new entrants to the workforce will be white males and nearly 85 percent will be women, minorities, and immigrants. "In 50 of America's 200

Intentional Diversity Transformation

cities with populations over 100,000, the so-called minority is the majority. Workers 55 and older are the fastest growing segment of the workforce. By some estimates, one in 10 Americans is gay. And technology is enabling more and more people with disabilities to enter the workforce".

The global marketplace has opened up a wide range of possibilities for organizational performance and success. Many organizations are broadening their potential markets beyond U.S. borders to include China, India, the Pacific Rim, all parts of Europe, South Africa, and the like. These organizations realize that differences in language, culture, processes, and business practices must be acknowledged to successfully enter these markets. In addition, they must learn from these diverse experiences and incorporate the skills, beliefs, and/or practices into organizational processes to capitalize on diversity for a competitive advantage.

One study by Poole highlights the following example: An American investment bank experienced problems when it launched an aggressive expansion plan into Europe. Their relocated American employees lacked credibility, were ignorant of local cultural norms and market conditions, and could not connect with their new clients. The investment bank responded to this problem by hiring Europeans

Intentional Diversity Transformation

who had attended North American business schools and assigning them in teams to the foreign offices. This strategy was enormously successful. The European operations were highly profitable and were staffed by a truly international group of professionals; however, the investment bank realized it still had a problem. If the French team, the German team, or the team in another country suddenly resigned, they would be right back where they were 10 years ago. The investment bank had not learned what the cultural differences really were or how they change the process of doing business. Cultural identity issues were never talked about openly. While they knew enough to use people's cultural strengths, they never internalized them or learned from them. Differences were valued, but they were not valued enough to be integrated into the organization's culture and business practices. In order to implement an effective diversity process, the investment bank needed to incorporate the extra steps to ensure that diversity was fully integrated into the organization's culture, skill sets, and functioning as a strategic capability issue.

Events such as mergers and acquisitions, changing customer marketplace demographics, and the like require organizations to work together. Organizations are also realizing that system flexibility, teamwork, measurement, and analysis is central to the

Intentional Diversity Transformation

drive for Six Sigma–level quality and innovation in products and services. Years of research have shown that well-managed, heterogeneous (diverse) groups will generally outperform homogeneous ones in problem solving, innovation, and creative solution building—exactly the capabilities that are critical to business success.

Organizations will have to be diverse because their customers are becoming more diverse, both abroad and in the United States. In the United States today, African Americans, Hispanics, Asian Americans, and Native Americans have an estimated combined spending power of more than $1.5 trillion. The shift to a service economy only increases the value of diverse employees, who may be better able to read and negotiate with such customers. The summary data below from the Selig Center for Economic Growth, Terry College of Business – The University of Georgia shows the spending power of minorities in the United States.

- **African-American buying power**, estimated at $1.2 trillion in 2016, will grow to $1.5 trillion by 2021, making it the largest racial minority consumer market. African-Americans constitute the nation's largest racial minority market; however, the buying power of Hispanics (an ethnic minority group) is larger. Black buying power increased 98

Intentional Diversity Transformation

percent from 2000 to 2016 and will comprise 8.8 percent of the nation's total buying power in 2021, according to the Selig Center.

- **Asian buying power** in 2014 was $770 billion and will rise to $1 trillion by 2019. Asian-Americans make up 6 percent of the population and control 6 percent of its purchasing power. Since 2000, Asian buying power has grown 222 percent to $891 billion, the biggest percentage increase of any U.S. minority group. U.S. Asian buying power exceeds the entire economies of all but 15 countries in the world. "The fast-paced growth of Asian consumers should create opportunities for businesses that pay attention to their needs and step in to serve niche markets,"

- **Hispanic buying power**. From a buying power estimate of $495 billion in 2000, the Hispanic group has increased its economic clout 181 percent to $1.4 trillion in 2016. That accounts for nearly 10 percent of total U.S. buying power in 2016 and means the U.S. Hispanic market is larger than the GDP of Mexico and bigger than the economies of all but 14 countries in the world.

- **Buying power of Native Americans** in 2014 was $100 billion, a 149 percent increase from 2000. The main reason for the increase in buying power for Native

Intentional Diversity Transformation

American's is an increase in population. For example, from 2000 through 2014, the Native American population grew by 48.9 percent.

Source: Publication - The Multicultural Economy 2017, Minority spending power in the U.S., Selig Center for Economic Growth, University of Georgia, Terry College of Business).

African-Americans constitute the nation's largest racial minority market; however, the buying power of Hispanics (an ethnic minority group) is larger. Black buying power increased 98 percent from 2000 to 2016 and will comprise 8.8 percent of the nation's total buying power in 2021, according to the Selig Center.

Failure to Implement a Diversity Initiative Can Be Costly

If the lures of increased productivity, global marketing effectiveness, improved problem-solving performance, and enhanced creativity are not enough to initiate change in your organization's culture, the downside risks and impacts of turnover costs, poor training return-on-investment due to short tenure, poor overall brand image, failing community image as a good place to work for all employees, litigation charges, and the like is certainly worth considering. It can cost as much as $112,000 to recruit and

Intentional Diversity Transformation

train a full-time sales employee with a salary of $100,000 per year. Other examples of retention costs include the following (Workplace News)

- $116,340 for a chief engineer with 17 years of service, earning $77,560 annually
- $110,000 for a government services underwriter with 11 years of service, earning $110,000 annually
- $105,000 for a vice president for 15 years of service, earning $63,000 annually
- $104,000 for a middle manager with 38 years of service, earning $52,000 annually
- $52,065 for a store manager with 21 years of service, earning $34,710 annually
- $44,888 for a shift foreperson with 14 years of service, earning $51,300 annually

In addition to these costs, there are lost productivity costs and dissatisfied client costs. Time, effort, and money must be spent on recruitment and selection to replace the employee who is leaving the organization. Lost productivity will result from the downtime created by the person leaving and the new employee's training and learning curve. Employees who are leaving, particularly those who believe they have not been treated fairly, are not likely to be overly

Intentional Diversity Transformation

productive after they hand in their resignations. New employees have to learn the job, the organizational structure, the formal rules, the informal rules, the workplace culture, and so on. This takes time. These downtimes could even result in an organization's product or service being delivered late—resulting in extremely dissatisfied customers.

Typically, replacement costs are at least 1.5 times the yearly salary of employees. Replacement costs for women and people of color are higher because the time-to-fill rate can be longer if the organization has poor candidate source pools. These costs do not account for lost accumulated company knowledge or low morale where turnover is high. Add to this a whole host of legislation (e.g., Family and Medical Leave Act, Americans with Disabilities Act, Age Discrimination in Employment Act, Immigration Reform and Control Act of 1986), the cost of litigation with judgments exceeding $1- 4 million, and the price of rebuilding a corporate image because of negative publicity, and some of the economic reasons for retaining employees become clear.

Diversity Links to Productivity and Performance

It is no secret that employees who are treated with respect and integrity and who are given an opportunity to have input into their work, on average, perform at higher levels. Employees figure out the level of effort they are required to put into their work. There is little doubt that satisfied employees are going to be better workers (i.e., their productivity will be higher than that of unsatisfied employees). In addition, fair employment practices allow organizations to more effectively attract, motivate, and retain the most qualified talent. Expectancy theory shows that treating employees fairly leads to higher levels of employee satisfaction and morale. An organization that has satisfied employees will find that it has low employee voluntary turnover (better known from an asset point of view as human capital depletion) and a highly productive workforce.

Research bears out the observation that employees who truly like their jobs and the organizations they work for tend to stay with the organization and have a positive impact on customer service and performance. One such body of research is the Service-Profit Chain developed by Haskett, Jones, Loveman, Sasser, and Schlesinger (1994). They established a causal pathway relationship that demonstrated that factors such as improving an organization's environment and an employee's satisfaction had a direct impact on customer satisfaction, retention, and loyalty, which generated a corresponding increase in organizational revenues and profits. In further research, Rucci, Quinn, and Kirn (1998) applied this Service-Profit Chain approach to organizational issues at Sears, Inc. and found that for every 5 percentage point improvement made in employee satisfaction, a 1.3 percentage point improvement in customer satisfaction and loyalty resulted, which drove a .5 percentage point improvement in store revenues. In one year, this accounted for an additional $200 million in revenue.

Employee satisfaction has a tremendous influence on employee commitment, which is reflected in key performance variables such as retention and productivity.

Retention

Employees will often cast their vote of dissatisfaction and level of commitment by using the "Law of Two Feet" (i.e., they go somewhere else). When this happens, it is usually already too late to recapture their commitment. Employees who are leaving, particularly those who believe they have not been treated fairly, are not likely to be overly productive after they hand in their resignations.

Intentional Diversity Transformation

It has been estimated that when an exempt (salaried) employee leaves an organization, it costs the organization 1.5 times the salary of the person who must be replaced. At the nonexempt (hourly) level, the impact is equivalent to 6 months of salary and benefits. It should also be noted that these figures only represent the costs needed to get a new person in the door! Costs incurred—such as learning curve costs, acculturation costs, formal and informal rules coaching, building customer and co-worker relationships, and network building costs equal to at least 90 percent of the departing employee—can represent a tremendous drain on the bottom line. These downtimes could even result in an organization's products and services being late—resulting in dissatisfied customers. This merely points out that it is critical that an organization manages employee retention and tracks who is leaving, for what reason, and at what cost.

When highly productive employees leave the organization, it can be disastrous. In many cases, high-performing employees are not allowed to work to their full potential because the workplace environment does not take employee differences and similarities into consideration as a competitive advantage. Dissatisfied employees will begin to look for work elsewhere. Under intense competition for the most qualified talent, an organization's ability

Intentional Diversity Transformation

to attract and retain high-caliber talent will depend in part on its reputation as an employer and whether employees are allowed to do their absolute personal best work. The consulting firm Deloitte & Touche, for example, found that it attracted more prospective employees after implementing Diversity initiatives. Both men and women stated that they wanted to work for a firm that is progressive and growing.

Conversely, a study conducted at a different workplace noted that women who do manage to get through the glass ceiling "feel so unsatisfied and undervalued that they leave early—and in proportionately greater numbers than their male counterparts." A study of 500 organizations found that nearly 40 percent of private-sector workers regularly think about quitting their jobs (Davis, 1996). Another workforce study showed that dissatisfied employees were three times more likely than satisfied employees to indicate their intent to leave the organization (Haskett et al., 1994). When these things occur, organizations jeopardize their ability to meet strategic business objectives.

Productivity

Another result of poor employee satisfaction is its impact on productivity. Drew Davis noted in a study of 500 organizations that downsized because they thought downsizing would reduce costs, increase productivity, and encourage people to work smarter, that these organizations experienced varying results. The fear of downsizing, eroding trust, disillusionment, and frustration about dwindling promotion opportunities and job security caused employees to be demotivated and bitter. This had a devastating hidden effect on the organization's bottom line. Seventy-five percent of the 500 organizations found that employee morale had collapsed, and two-thirds of these organizations showed no increase in efficiency.

Productivity relates not only to direct effort but also to discretionary effort. This relates to the extra effort that employees give to their work. In today's workplaces, discretionary effort can make the difference between getting and not getting a client and between keeping and losing a client. Many organizations can replicate their competitors' technology, but they cannot replicate their workforces. In an information- and intellectual capital–based society, competitive organizational capability will come through people—people who are valued regardless of their backgrounds and who are given the opportunity to be innovative and fully productive. Demotivated, non-valued employees will rarely expend the extra effort that may be required to win over customers and gain a competitive advantage.

Diverse work teams have been found to possess the potential to achieve higher levels of performance than homogeneous teams. Diverse groups of people bring a broad range of skills, knowledge, abilities, and perspectives to organizational challenges. Research has shown that diverse teams frequently develop more ideas and potential solutions to problems than homogeneous teams. Capowski described studies of four organizations: AT&T, Harris Bank, Northrup Grumman, and GE Power Systems. They found that the performance of the diverse work teams generated more ideas that evolved into new products and services than the performance of homogeneous teams. The latter group does not have as many perspectives to bring to the table as a diverse work team. The synergy that can be created by a homogeneous group of people is limited because they are so similar. With the proper training, diverse work teams can make the most of their varied perspectives and outperform homogeneous teams; however, homogeneous teams do come to the table with a common frame of reference, and they know how to communicate effectively with each other.

Intentional Diversity Transformation

Members of a diverse team are unlikely to have that knowledge and often must be trained in specific processes and techniques that effectively utilize their varied perspectives. To ensure effectiveness, team members must understand their differences, the communication process, group dynamics, and ways to integrate their many ideas into cohesive solutions. Diversity can "breed tension, conflict, misunderstandings, and frustration unless an organization develops a culture that supports, honors, and values differences" (Van Eron).

In the following examples, Addison Reid illustrates the impact of diversity on the bottom line of two organizations:

Example One. A Spanish speaker in the decision-making loop could have saved General Motors the expense of trying to market the Chevy Nova in Mexico. Nova is Spanish for "it doesn't go."

Example Two. If Gerber baby foods had known the local customs, it would have been saved the expense of recalling and relabeling jars and apologizing to its clients in one African country for suggesting that they were cannibals (nobody feed ground-up babies in a jar to other babies as the label implied!). In that country, it is customary for a label to picture the product, not the intended client. Gerber, in its attempt to address Diversity, had simply

Intentional Diversity Transformation

changed the white baby on the label of their baby food jars to a black baby.

In both cases, this lack of Diversity awareness and diversity utilization cost the organizations millions of dollars in lost revenue and damage to its brand image—not to mention its major impact on productivity costs.

The Link Between the Lack of Diversity Programs and Absenteeism

Productivity is directly affected by the cost of absenteeism and hostile work environments. Satisfied employees are absent less often than unsatisfied employees, are late less often, are less apt to leave early, and are less apt to use expensive short-term and long-term disability benefits. Employees witnessing and/or experiencing hostile work environments and harassment are often away more often and are less productive. Imperial Oil of Canada estimates that harassment costs them close to $8 million annually in absenteeism, employee turnover, and loss of productivity. This does not include legal fees (Poole). This is a high price to pay for something that can be prevented.

Intentional Diversity Transformation

If employees are staying with the organization and working well, customers are more apt to be happy and satisfied. While employee turnover costs money and time for recruiting, hiring, and training replacements, it also affects customer satisfaction. The employee who left, for example, may have been in contact with the organization's customers, and the customers will now have to deal with someone new who does not understand their needs. The customer, more than likely, may have been satisfied with the employee who just left. This employee may have been their primary contact with the organization for the past five or so years. He or she knew the customer's special needs. Now the customer will have to deal with the new employee or choose to go somewhere else. An even more frightening scenario is that the customers follow the employee who is leaving your organization (who knows all of the company's secrets) to your competitor, taking their business with them.

One study showed that low employee turnover was found to be linked closely to high customer satisfaction. The study found that when an employee who had direct contact with a customer left, their customer satisfaction level dropped sharply from 75 percent to 55 percent (Haskett et al., 1994). Another study by Abt Associates concluded that there was an average monthly cost of $36,000 in sales for replacing a sales representative with five to eight years of experience with an employee who had less than one year of experience. Conservative estimates of replacing a broker at a securities firm concluded that it takes nearly five years for a broker to rebuild relationships with customers that can return $1 million per year in commissions to the brokerage house, which amounts to a cumulative loss of at least $2.5 million in commission (Haskett et al., 1994).

Customers who know that their needs are going to be met are usually satisfied customers; however, as Janet Lapp (1996) points out, cynicism has developed among customers about what to expect from organizations. Many customers have low expectations about the ability of organizations to do what they say they will do or to be different from their competitors in a meaningful way. In order to be successful, organizations should be looking for ways to build strong, solid reputations for delivery and working to sustain the loyalty of their customers. Lapp points out that the "CEO of Starbucks believes that the quality of his workforce is the company's only sustainable, competitive advantage. He believes that workers need to feel pride in and to have a stake in the outcome of their efforts on the job." In essence, they must feel valued and included in the work climate and the decisions that affect their lives.

Intentional Diversity Transformation

Diversity's Contribution to the Bottom Line

Satisfied customers tend to be loyal customers; not many satisfied customers go to the competition. One way of ensuring that customers are satisfied is to have a workforce that clearly reflects the organization's marketplace. This has become clear in the banking industry. Most banks, for example, offer about the same rates; it is the people who make the difference—the customer service difference (Martinez, 1995). We know from past experience that satisfied and loyal customers often become life-long customers bringing repeat business. Not only will this repeat business boost revenues, but satisfied and loyal customers will also make referrals. Referrals are one of the best ways to increase an organization's customer base and, in turn, its profitability. This includes direct referrals as well as pass-along referrals, where the customer brags about your organization and customers show up without any intervention (e.g., marketing, sales efforts) on your part. Satisfied customers also make excellent references when your business calls for them in a bidding situation. Good references can make the difference between being an unsuccessful bidder and winning the contract! Conversely, a dissatisfied customer can severely damage your organization's reputation and can affect future sales and profits.

Intentional Diversity Transformation

In general, whenever an organization experiences customer-base growth, it translates into a better bottom line, increasing sales and profits. One study by Reicheld and Sasser (1990) found that a 5 percent increase in customer loyalty can produce profit increases that range from 25 to 85 percent. Organizations can determine customer loyalty by tracking customer retention, the number of services used by each customer, and the level of customer satisfaction. The strategies derived from this information helped explain why one of the organizations studied had achieved a return on assets in recent years more than double that of its competitors (Haskett et al., 1994).

Organizations that have included diversity in their organizational goals realize the importance of investing in their employees and servicing the varying needs of their customers. Increases in profits give organizations an opportunity to spend more time and money to make certain the workplace meets the needs of all workers while providing a fair return to shareholders.

Organizations that do not have an effective Diversity process or no process at all will also incur costs, including high turnover, low morale, ineffective products or services, unproductive teams, inability to attract and retain employees, and legal and other

Intentional Diversity Transformation

expenses. Some well-known discrimination and bias cases from the past that illustrate this impact on the bottom line, however, in many ways, we still have not fully learned the lesson they generated and seem destined to repeat them. These cases included the following:

- Coca-Cola ($192.5M) Race
- State Farm ($250M) Gender
- Home Depot ($110M) Gender
- Lucky Stores ($107M) Gender
- Publix ($82M) Gender
- Texaco ($176M) Race
- Shoneys ($132M) Race
- Denny's ($54M) Race

Poorly implemented Diversity processes can damage an organization's reputation with current and future (potential) employees as well as current and future customers and investors. An effective process, on the other hand, will increase the organization's goodwill and reputation (Poole). By effectively measuring and tracking the costs and benefits of diversity, organizations truly understand that Diversity is a bottom-line business issue that is critical to organizational performance and results.

Intentional Diversity Transformation

Building Centers of Diversity Excellence

Conducting diversity work as a strategic partner is some of the most important work we can do. It is critical to the myriad of customers served and vital to the people utilized inside the organization that diversity supports. Learning to serve as a strategic partner within the organizational structure is not just a way for Diversity practitioners to justify their existence or defend their turf. It has implications for the very survival of the diversity department and of the organization as a whole. If the Diversity function cannot show that it adds value, it risks being on the table for reduction, or worse—dismantling. With the right diversity mindset and measurement tools, implementing diversity-strategic business objectives can mean the critical difference between an organization that is just keeping pace with the competition or one that is making major strides ahead. In essence, it requires creating centers of Diversity excellence using behavioral and technical ROI measurement capability, demonstrating commitment, and building communities of practice to sustain it over time.

In order for an organization to take full advantage of the potential wealth in its Diversity mixtures, it must completely embrace the level of Diversity required to meet critical organizational challenges head on. This occurs when organizations foster a climate and culture

Intentional Diversity Transformation

that values differences and maximizes the potential of employees through utilization—in other words, when the organization and the individuals within it operate in a mature fashion.

According to Dr. R. Roosevelt Thomas (1999), Diversity-maturity requires both an individual and organizational set of behaviors that drive success. He states that Diversity-mature individuals do the following:

- Accept personal responsibility for enhancing their own and their organization's effectiveness.
- Demonstrates contextual knowledge (i.e., they know themselves and their organizations and they understand key diversity concepts and definitions).
- Are clear about requirements and base include/exclude decisions about differences on how they impact the ability to meet these requirements.
- Understand that Diversity is accompanied by complexity and tension and are prepared to cope with these in pursuit of greater Diversity effectiveness.
- Are willing to challenge conventional wisdom.
- Engage in continuous learning.

Intentional Diversity Transformation

Diversity-mature individuals see themselves, not others, as responsible for addressing Diversity effectively. They understand the impact of organizational culture on Diversity-related practices, but they do not use it as an excuse for inaction and indifference. Thomas points out that individuals aiming for greater Diversity effectiveness would do well to ask themselves the following personal Diversity questions:

- Am I comfortable working with people from all demographic groups?
- Is there a group or groups that I struggle to accept? If so, how have I attempted to overcome my biases?
- How will my comfort or lack of comfort with people different from me affect my ability to advance within this workplace?
- Do I enjoy Diversity? If so, what kind? If so, how much?

Diversity professionals are not exempt from these issues and must answer these questions for themselves. Diversity-mature individuals know that when people with different backgrounds, perspectives, and objectives express themselves openly, there will be tension. This tension is not inherently positive or negative, good or bad; it simply is. Tension that promotes healthy competition can be good. Tension that immobilizes a unit is clearly not. The difficulty is that many individuals, like organizations, are so uncomfortable with tension that they focus on eliminating it rather than managing it. They place more importance on harmony than on achieving objectives.

Diversity-mature individuals learn to function in the face of tension. They know it is not personal but rather part and parcel of the dynamics of diversity. Tension and conflict are not the same. Tension becomes conflict when it is responded to ineptly. Diversity conflict arises when people ask unproductive questions, such as, "What's wrong with you that you aren't more like me?" (Thomas, 1999). Diversity-mature individuals have challenged conventional wisdom and made mindset changes along the way that equip them to respond effectively to these challenges.

By adjusting to this new mindset and accepting personal responsibility for action, diversity practitioners can develop new competencies to fulfill their strategic roles. The new economic paradigm of diversity as a financial contributor requires diversity professionals to do different things and help the organization deal with the dynamic tension that comes with managing a diverse workforce. This means more than just understanding the organization's articulated strategy; it means that Diversity

Intentional Diversity Transformation

professionals must become strategic business partners who comprehend exactly what capabilities, environments, and other factors are needed to drive successful strategy implementation in their organizations and the ways in which Diversity affects these components.

To create this center of Diversity excellence, diversity-mature individuals must be able to let go of hindering concepts, such as only people with good interpersonal skills can be successful in managing diversity. Good interpersonal skills help, but they are not the sole arbiters of success. Diversity-mature individuals are highly capable of unlearning when needed. Diversity effectiveness requires a willingness and ability to monitor both yourself and the environment, to challenge yourself regularly, and to devise specific ways to work with new concepts so that they eventually become second nature (Thomas, 1999).

To create excellence in performance (utilizing diversity), diversity professionals must possess core Diversity skills, which are implemented from a strategic framework. These skills, among others, include the following:

- *Ability to identify diversity mixtures and their related tensions.* Because unidentified mixtures cannot be addressed, this is a critical skill. On the surface this skill seems simple and straightforward, yet according to Thomas (1999), many people fail to master it. There is a natural tendency to focus on the diversity mixture that is of most interest to them and to ignore the others. People often overemphasize one Diversity dimension such as race or gender at the expense of identifying a critical mixture that may have the most impact on organizational performance.

- *Ability to analyze mixtures and related tensions.* Not all mixtures need to be addressed, only those that interfere with achieving the goal. How key is the mixture? How disruptive are the tensions? Is any action needed? If action is taken, will it significantly enhance meeting the organizational objectives?
- *Ability to select an appropriate response.* If action is needed, what should the action be? In *Redefining Diversity* (1996), Thomas suggests responses from a framework that identifies at least eight choices, including increase/decrease, deny, assimilate, suppress, isolate, tolerate, build future relationships or foster mutual adaptation. Diversity professionals who are skilled in using these responses can quickly sort through the possible options and select the most effective one.

Intentional Diversity Transformation

To be effective, Diversity professionals must demonstrate a kind of diversity maturity that allows them to internalize key Diversity concepts and use them to guide their actions along with integrating the core skills.

Similarly, to be effective at Diversity measurement, individuals aiming for greater Diversity measurement effectiveness would do well to ask themselves some critical personal questions:

- Am I comfortable with working with metrics and evaluating data from all demographic groups?
- Are there concepts around measuring diversity, especially beyond race and gender, that I struggle to accept? If so, how have I attempted to overcome my biases?
- How will my comfort or lack of comfort with metrics affect my ability to utilize them within this workplace?
- Do I enjoy Diversity measurement? If so, what kind? If so, how much?
- Do I need to hire someone to conduct this portion of our strategic Diversity impact analysis or simply support our efforts as a reviewer?
- Do I really want to do the real work required to rigorously apply Diversity measures and following the

Intentional Diversity Transformation

Diversity return-on-investment (DROI®) process through to its conclusion?

Answers to these questions will help identify any baseline resistance to the Diversity measurement process. Sometimes biases toward diversity measurement can come from within our profession and impede setting standards of excellence.

To sustain Diversity professionals' momentum for excellence and measurement, communities of practice are required. What is a Diversity measurement community of practice? It is a group of people who share a concern, set of problems, or a passion for identifying the impact of diversity using measurement processes and who deepen their knowledge and expertise in this area by learning about Diversity measurement and interacting on an ongoing basis. They find it useful to compare designs regularly and to discuss the intricacies of their area of interest in Diversity measurement. Currently, the Hubbard Diversity Measurement and Productivity Institute (HDM&P) and the Hubbard Diversity Return on Investment Institutes operate communities of practice focused on Diversity analytics and ROI measurement called the Diversity Return on Investment (DROI) Forum.

Intentional Diversity Transformation

As communities of practice, these people do not necessarily work together every day, but they meet as strategic business partners because they find value in their interactions. As they spend time together, they typically share information, insight, and advice. They help each other solve problems. They discuss their diversity measurement situations, their aspirations, and their needs. They ponder issues, explore ideas, and act as sounding boards. They may create tools, standards, generic designs, manuals, and other documents. However they accumulate knowledge, they become informally bound by the value they find in learning about diversity measurement together. This value is not merely instrumental for their work. It also accrues in personal satisfaction of knowing colleagues who understand each other's perspectives and of belonging to a group of people who enjoy the diversity measurement work. Over time, they develop a unique perspective on the topic as well as a body of common knowledge, practices, and approaches. They may even develop a common sense of identity (Wenger, McDermott, Snyder, 2002). They become a diversity measurement community of practice.

Intentional Diversity Transformation

Final Thoughts

An effective, measurable business case for Diversity must be built on a solid framework of both concept and science through the work of competent, credible Diversity professionals using clear standards of excellence linked to business performance. They must view Diversity as an integral part of the organizational system. By integrating the ideas underlying Diversity with specific measurement strategies and organizational systems theory, Diversity professionals can help the organization examine and utilize its diverse resources more dynamically. It is, of course, impossible to predict future events and results; however, we can make better decisions for the future by using tools such as the Diversity Scorecard to guide us and to test alternatives as a basis for discussing how the future might look.

References

Addison Reid, Barbara. "Mentorships Ensure Equal Opportunity." *Personnel Journal*, November 1994, 122–123.

Baytos, Lawrence M. *Designing & Implementing Successful Diversity Programs*. Englewood Cliffs, NJ: Prentice Hall, 1995.

Becker, Brian E., Mark A. Huselid, and Dave Ulrich. *The HR Scorecard: Linking People, Strategy, and Performance*. Boston: Harvard Business School Press, 2001.

Capowski, Genevieve. "Managing Diversity." *Management Review*, 85: 13–19.

Cox, Taylor Jr. *Cultural Diversity in Organizations*. San Francisco: Berrett-Koehler, 1993.

Cox, Taylor, Jr., and Ruby L Beale. *Developing Competency to Manage Diversity*. San Francisco: Berrett-Koehler, 1997.

Davis, Drew. "Beyond Casual Fridays: Are Managers Tuned in to Workplace Culture?" *Canadian HR Reporter*, May 6, 1996, 17.

Haskett, James L., Thomas O. Jones, Gary W. Loveman, Earl W. Sasser, Jr., and Leonard A Schlesinger. "Putting the Service-Profit Chain to Work." *Harvard Business Review*, March/April 1994, 164–174.

Haskett, James L., Earl W. Sasser, Jr., and Leonard A. Schlesinger. *The Service Profit Chain*. New York: The Free Press, 1997.

Hubbard, Edward E. *How to Calculate Diversity Return on Investment*. Petaluma, CA: Global Insights, 1999.

Hubbard, Edward E. *Measuring Diversity Results*. Petaluma, CA: Global Insights, 1997.

IBM and Towers Perrin. *Priorities for Competitive Advantage*. New York: IBM and Towers Perrin, 1991.

Kaplan, Robert S., and David P. Norton. *The Balanced Scorecard*. Boston: Harvard Business School Press, 1996.

Lapp, Janet. *Plant Your Feet Firmly in Mid-Air*. Albany, NY: Delmar, 1996.

Loden, Marilyn. *Implementing Diversity*. Chicago: Irwin, 1996.

Loden, Marilyn, and Judith Rosener. *Workforce America*. Homewood, IL: Business One Irwin, 1991.

Martinez, Michelle Neely. "Equality Effort: Sharpens Bank's Edge." *HR Magazine*, January 1995, 38–43.

Poole, Phebe-Jane. *Diversity: A Business Advantage*. Ajax, Ontario: Poole Publishing, 1997.

Reichheld, Frederick F., and Earl W. Sasser, Jr. "Zero Defections: Quality Comes to Services." *Harvard Business Review*, October 1990.

Rucci, Anthony J., Steven P. Kirn, and Richard T. Quinn. "The Employee-Customer-Profit Chain at Sears." *Harvard Business Review*, 76(1):1998, 90.

Thomas, R. Roosevelt, Jr. *Beyond Race and Gender*. New York: AMACOM, 1991.

Thomas, R. Roosevelt, Jr. *Building a House for Diversity*. New York: AMACOM, 1999.

Thomas, R. Roosevelt, Jr. *Redefining Diversity*. New York: AMACOM, 1996.

See "No More Business as Usual," *Working Woman*, Special Advertising Section: Strength Through Diversity for Bottom-line Success: A Call to Manage Diversity. MacDonald Communications Corporation, March 1999.

Von Eron, Ann M. "Ways to Assess Diversity Success." *HR Magazine*, August 1995, 51–60.

Wenger, Etienne, Richard McDermott, and William M. Snyder. *Cultivating Communities of Practice*. Boston: Harvard Business School Press, 2002.

Chapter Three: Introduction to Diversity Measurement

It's All Subjective . . . or Is It?

There seems to be a myth operating within business and governmental communities that suggests that the outcomes or results created by a Diversity change process defy measurement or can only be measured in the long term. In a sense, this myth suggests that creating an effective Diversity-mature work environment is something of a complex and mysterious art form. Allegedly, the real value of diversity work can only be judged by those who perform it, those who are truly committed to its purpose or value it as important. Even then, the assessment of the results is saddled with subjectivity.

Some Diversity specialists perceive that an inherent conflict exists between what is good for business and what is good for people. Some others believe, like truth, that the real reward is in the work itself. The words used to describe the results often include terms

Intentional Diversity Transformation

such as working better, appreciating differences, understanding each other better, less conflict, getting along, working as a team, and other similar non-measurement-specific words. Although these are admirable aims in themselves, they are not enough, especially when organizations are looking for strategies to deal with increased competition, options for reducing cost, adding value, adding dollars, and increasing productivity to affect the bottom line.

These notions seem to imply that quantifiable and quality-based measures cannot be applied to the Diversity implementation process or a diverse work culture. Some people even believe that Diversity is not a business-focused activity, but simply another form of affirmative action regulatory compliance, even though demographics, which are irrefutable, have been set in motion that show Diversity is not only a business and customer issue but also a global competitive issue!

Whether the subjective position is valid is a key question to be sure; however, just the fact that it exists and that some Diversity professionals and other businesspeople support it creates major problems. It sets managing and leveraging diversity apart from the rest of the organization. While peers in other organizational areas are focusing on metrics that reflect their contribution, such as sales, reduced costs, profits, income and expenses, and so on, those implementing the Diversity process may limit its contribution to increased awareness, improved feelings, and increased satisfaction among groups. It is a real missed opportunity.

Some line managers quickly make judgments about diversity being a soft, non-business-oriented endeavor that contributes little to bottom-line performance. In addition, these managers may also assume that those involved in diversity neither understand nor are interested in measuring Diversity's contribution to the organization. As a result, diversity is not taken seriously. Fewer managers support it in actual practice by sending their workforce to be trained or structuring their workforce to leverage diversity mixtures through teaming or implementing multicultural marketing strategies that penetrate key ethnic customer markets, and so on. We know from current organizational practice that Diversity initiatives result in fewer follow-throughs than other business initiatives. Many Diversity professionals resent this second-hand treatment, yet it is inevitable given the lack of a common connection and language that is fundamental to business.

There is no escaping numbers. Without them the line departments would have little idea of their performance. Also, it would be impossible to report back to stakeholders and stockholders. This being the case, how does the Diversity department or professional exist in this climate? Some surveys of human resource professionals in general show that although they knew the number of employees in the company, "[a] majority of major corporation human resource professionals couldn't state the dollar volume of sales for their company, didn't know the profit level, and had little idea of the rate of return on corporate dollars invested" (Fitz-enz, 1995).

These issues are all part of the daily lives of line managers. The conclusion is somewhat obvious: If Diversity professionals want to be effective communicators, they must build rapport with their audiences. The most direct way to do this is by recognizing their audience's values and using their language to communicate—the language of numbers.

Reasons for Lack of Quantification in Diversity

There are several reasons why quantification in Diversity is lacking. Probably the most prevalent is that diversity professionals simply do not know how to objectively measure diversity activities.
The focus on diverse workforce management and development is still relatively new, and there are many methods to implement

Intentional Diversity Transformation

Diversity and the process of diverse workforce development. Many diversity professionals are still trying to understand all of the implications of diverse workforce trends in the national and global arena. Because there are few predecessors, it is not surprising that many Diversity professionals still rely on subjective measures.

Some practitioners in the Diversity field have human resources backgrounds and have had the opportunity to study human resource development in college. Unfortunately, statistical courses are not always a part of many human resource development curricula. Even when they are, they tend to be either financial or behavioral science methods. Statistical procedures have seldom been adapted to the creation of input-output ratios for measuring diversity processes or the results of a human resources function. The reason for this is fairly simple: Many of the academic processes have never really been applied to the problem. Little formal training in Diversity metrics existed before the founding of the HDM&P Institute.

The second reason behind the subjectivity myth is the values conflict. Some believe that objective measurement is simply inappropriate for diversity work. In their eyes, Diversity work is a function devoted to stimulating and supporting human development, and they see no reason to evaluate outcomes in other than humanitarian terms. This one-sided approach is prevalent in many occupations. Some managers believe the sole mission of training is to transfer technical information about work from one person's brain into the brains of the workers. This is the technical competency model of human development. They see no real responsibility to teach workers to think, evaluate, or form values. Some architects, for example, believe their job is to create a container within which some kind of activity can be efficiently carried out. They overlook the fact that human beings interact with the space and can be depressed or stimulated by it. These perspectives ignore the holistic philosophies of systemic organizational views.

For those whose value system conflicts with the notion of measuring diversity, there is little hope for change—unless they experience a significant emotional event like losing their diversity position, funding, and/or support because it is thought that very little value is derived from their diversity work. Even then, some people still may not get it. Until they expand their outlook to include supporting the strategic purpose of the organization, there will be the perception that management should just see this as a good thing or the right thing to do.

Another very common reason why Diversity departments or diversity activities are not measured is that some Diversity

Intentional Diversity Transformation

professionals fear measurement. Perhaps this notion is born out of a fear of knowing; however, if you don't know, you can almost guarantee that nothing will ever improve. But what if you're making terrific progress and don't know it? What if several areas were doing a great job in utilizing the Diversity mixtures of their work groups but are beginning to slip back into old, less effective habits? Key opportunities for adjustment and reinforcement would be missed. The implications of this can be mind boggling. This brings us to the fourth and last reason for the subjectivity myth.

Some members of top management have bought the myth of subjectivity—but not for long! Perhaps this is because for a long time there has been little interest in human resources issues. The early captains of industry simply never asked the question. As time progressed, the tradition of non-measurability went unchallenged. Few CEOs have taken more than a cursory tour in the human resources or diversity department during their careers. It was often just a quick stop along the way to the executive suite. Just about the time they were beginning to sink their teeth into what could be accomplished and what may need to be changed, they were off to another developmental assignment. Many of these budding executives, knowing the assignment would be a brief 12 to 18 months, looked for quick projects with a lot of visibility. Very few embarked on major, fundamental projects that would touch all facets of human resource issues.

Today this attitude is changing. Rotational developmental assignments in diversity are being given to high-potential movers and shakers as part of their development. Certainly all of the glass ceilings have not been shattered, but they are beginning to break in organizations that are serious about understanding and utilizing diversity as a key competitive strategy. Part of the Diversity professional's hesitation is in the challenges of quantification.

Challenges of Quantification

GTE (now part of Verizon) has been a leader in efforts to develop measures of intangible assets such as human capital. The firm has recognized both the limitations of traditional accounting measures for intangible assets and the potential represented by a more balanced performance measurement system. According to Lawrence R. Whitman, deputy CFO at GTE, "[a] direct link between human capital and corporate financial results is not readily apparent in traditional accounting practices. Right now, we are only beginning to understand the potential of this tool, but it's the measurement process that's important. . . . Once we are able to measure intangible assets more accurately, I think investors and finance professionals will begin to look at human capital metrics as another indicator of a company's value" (Becker, Huselid, Ulrich, 2001).

Certainly, at a gut level, people may have an inclination that having diverse human capital in a diverse and/or global marketplace may be beneficial, but how is it really? When we speak of measurement as a strategic resource for Diversity professionals and others, what do we really mean? For example, many firms identify one or two people-related measures, such as employee satisfaction, in a balanced set of measures of organizational performance. Line managers, even Diversity managers, might be held accountable for these measures, which could be incorporated into an executive bonus plan. These measures capture the quantity, or level, of a particular attribute—in this case, employee satisfaction—but how much is there? Does it change over time? How does it compare with the employee satisfaction experienced at other organizations or across strategic business units (SBUs)? Most of us would simply *assume* that more employee satisfaction is a good thing for the organization because organizations often have very little real *evidence* supporting this link between employee satisfaction and organizational performance. Such organizations emphasize the level of the attribute, rather than the *relationship* between the attribute and some strategic outcome, such as performance drivers or the organization's performance.

Good measurement requires an understanding of and expertise in measuring both levels and relationships. Too many Diversity professionals succumb to pressures to demonstrate diversity's link to performance by merely relying on *levels* of Diversity outcomes as substitutes for measures of *relationship*. In other words, they cannot show the direct causal links between diversity outcomes and the organization's performance, so they select several plausible Diversity or human resource measures as candidates for strategic drivers, then simply assert their connection to the organization's performance.

This inability to demonstrate these relationships is sometimes obscured by diagrams that vaguely suggest cause and effect, as shown in the following diagram:

Intentional Diversity Transformation

This diagram shows a common example of what might be called a superficial strategy map. A firm might include one or two measures under each of these three categories and do a good job of measuring the levels of those attributes. But what does doing well on those measures really mean? The arrows imply that better performance on the People dimension improves performance on the Customer dimension, which in turn will improve Profits. But the real story of value creation in any firm is much more complicated, so the story is incomplete (Becker, Huselid, Ulrich, 2001). It provides only the most superficial guide to decision making or performance evaluation. It is only marginally better than traditional measures that make no effort to incorporate a larger strategic role for diversity. Boxes and arrows give the illusion of measurement and understanding, but because the *relationship* measures are so limited, such diagrams and the thinking behind them can actually undermine the confidence and credibility the organization has for Diversity processes.

Even though relationship measurement is the most compelling assessment challenge facing Diversity professionals today, attribute measures should form the foundation of a measurement system. Why? Because evidence of a strong relationship between A and B is worthless if the measures of A and B themselves are worthless. But words such as "worthless" or "useful" or "appropriate" are not precise enough for a discussion about the elements of good measurement. In fact, there are well-defined principles outlining effective measurement practice. Understanding those principles lets the Diversity professional take that essential step forward in developing a strategically focused Diversity measurement system. Let's briefly explore a few of these principles.

The Definition of Measurement

Measurement is defined as the assignment of numbers to properties (or characteristics) of objects based on a set of rules. Because we are often interested in the quantities related to a Diversity outcome, numerical representation is important; however, we are not

Intentional Diversity Transformation

interested in just any quantities—we want the quantities to have meaning. For example, if we conduct a diverse workforce climate survey and ask the question: *"My* manager/supervisor knows how to work with a diverse workforce," knowing that the average score is 3.5 on a 5-point scale is numerical does not have much inherent meaning. Is scoring 3.5 good or bad? Or consider an employee turnover rate of 15 percent. Percentage points have more inherent meaning than 5-point scales, but simply observing the number does not reveal much about whether 15 percent is a problem.

To add meaning to these levels, we need to add context. This is the appeal of a benchmark. If we find our 3.5 on a 5-point scale is considerably better than our industry peers' ratings, we can begin to attach some significance to that measure; however, we might observe that our 3.5 is considerably below our historical level on this measure. We are doing better than our peers but not maintaining our historical performance. Of course, in both cases we have made interpretations about the relative value only (i.e., we are better or worse than some standard). In neither case do we have any measure of managerial value. In other words, what difference does it make whether we have a 3.0 or 4.0 value on a 5-point diverse workforce climate survey? To have managerial value, the measure must be expressed in numerical units that have inherent performance

Intentional Diversity Transformation

significance (such as a dollar impact). Barring that, we have to be able to translate the measure into performance-relevant units.

Let's take a look at another example: Suppose you want to demonstrate the dollar impact cost (recruitment and retention costs, lower productivity) associated with each additional percentage point in your organization's diverse workforce turnover numbers. To get managerial value out of this exercise, you would have to link diversity measures to performance drivers in other parts of the organization and ultimately to the organization's overall performance. Remember the finding from Sears in the previous chapter, where Sears put the Service-Profit Chain to work. The key people measures in the Sears measurement model reflect employees' attitudes toward their jobs and the organization overall. Sears could have benchmarked those attitudes against similar levels at other companies or perhaps against Sears' own historical norms. From this, the organization might have identified a gap, but then it would have to ask, so what? Unlike most companies, Sears had an answer to this question because it could translate changes in those attitude measures into changes in the organization's performance. Therefore, the people numbers had a business meaning.

Intentional Diversity Transformation

Measuring relationships gives meaning to the levels and to potential changes in those levels; however, those relationships are very likely to be organization specific. Therefore, the more these (the impact of one measure on another) relationships are unique to your organization, the less useful it will be for your organization to benchmark on these levels with other organizations. Benchmarking on measurement levels assumes that the relationships among these levels are the same in all firms, and thus they have the same meaning in all organizations. That is the same as saying that the strategy implementation process is a commodity. For this reason, benchmarking on diversity strategic measures can be misguided at best and counterproductive at worst.

In addition, to fully understand another measurement principle, it is helpful to examine the differences between measures versus concepts or visions. To effectively measure Diversity, our focus should be on the structure and value-creating elements of the Diversity measurement system. These elements show up as Diversity deliverables and the organization's key performance drivers that the deliverables influence. We can think of these properties as abstract concepts but also as observable measures. First, an organization or top management team can identify key links in the value-creation chain by taking what might be called a conceptual or vision perspective. For example, the simple relationship between employee attitudes and the organization's performance serves as the foundation of the Sears measurement model discussed earlier. Sears refined its model further with brief vision statements about the important attributes of each element in its model. The Sears top management team felt that Sears must be a *compelling* place to work, a *compelling* place to shop, and a *compelling* place to invest (the three C's).

This kind of concept or vision, commonly referred to as *constructs*, is the property of the organization's strategy implementation process; however, constructs are so abstract that they provide very little guidance for decision making or performance evaluation. For example, identifying superior cross-selling performance in ethnic markets as a key performance driver may get you closer to an effective assessment beyond the vision stage, but it is still too conceptual to be operational. What does it mean? How will we know it if we see it? Will two different managers both know it when they see it? In short, how do we measure it?

Compelling and easy-to-grasp constructs are important because they help you capture and communicate the essence of powerful ideas. Nevertheless, they are not measures. Rather, they constitute the foundation on which you *build* your measures. Clarifying a construct is the first step in understanding your organization's value-creation story, but you must then know how to move beyond the construct to the level of measure.

One way to detect a good measure is to see how accurately it reflects its underlying construct. Earlier, we said that a measure of the relationship between A and B is worthless. A or B would be worthless if they did not reflect the constructs behind them. For example, if Sears measured the construct "compelling place to work" simply by assessing the level of employee satisfaction with pay, the measure would not have very much relevance. Why? Because it omits key dimensions, such as understanding business strategy or relationships with supervisors, of the underlying idea that it is designed to tap (Becker, Huselid, Ulrich, 2001).

One way to avoid this kind of mistake is to use multiple measures that reflect different dimensions of the same construct. In Sears' case, managers used a 70-item survey that they then distilled to 10 items along two dimensions: employee attitudes about the job and employee attitudes about the company (see Figure).

Intentional Diversity Transformation

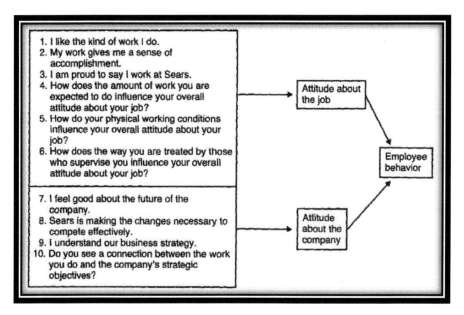

Figure: Survey of employee attitudes. Responses to these 10 questions on a 70-question employee survey had a higher impact on employee behavior (and, therefore, on customer satisfaction) than the measures that were devised initially: *personal growth* and *empowerment teams*. (Source: *The HR Scorecard: Linking People, Strategy, and Performance*, 2001.)

This approach gave the organization an explicit way to assess how well it was realizing its vision of being a compelling place to work.

Another problem that can arise when choosing metrics is that of contamination. This means the measure does not correspond to its underlying construct. Often, this can happen for at least two reasons:

Intentional Diversity Transformation

(1) the measure does not fully capture all of the properties of the construct, or (2) the measure is capturing something beyond the construct. This is an all-too-common error. Remember the example discussed previously identifying superior cross-selling performance in ethnic markets as a key performance driver? How should the organization measure this construct? It might use total sales at all divisions, under the assumption that employees and divisions with more cross-selling skills in ethnic markets would have higher total sales. But total sales would also include sales other than those derived from cross-selling and those other than from ethnic markets by employees. The other data in each case would contaminate the metric. What about assessing total number of different products sold per customer or new sales to existing customers in ethnic markets? In either case, the organization would still have to develop a measure that tapped into the important attribute of the performance driver in question without blurring the picture with unrelated influences.

These sorts of measurement errors severely reduce the value you can derive from your diversity measurement system. If you use deficient measures, it is very likely that the organization will begin to ignore—or worse, misrepresent—the diversity link to the performance driver. For example, if a key driver is positive customer buying experience, you might use time with customer as a measure.

Market research shows that customers appreciate it when sales staffs do not pressure them to make a quick purchase. On the other hand, if this is the *only* measure of the customer's buying experience, salespeople might be tempted to needlessly drag out their encounters with customers. It is still true that what gets measured, gets managed. Simply put, we cannot measure A and hope for B (Becker, Huselid, Ulrich, 2001).

Outcome Measures or Performance Drivers?

In a balanced scorecard, outcome measures are combined with measures that describe resources spent or activities performed. We are interested in how the measures will help us track the outcomes of one Diversity initiative and how it drives the performance of a key aspect of the organization's business. By focusing on performance drivers, we emphasize that we want to measure those factors that will determine or influence future outcomes.

Goals and measures can be placed in a traditional input-output model to illustrate how goals and measures may be placed along a causal chain, from resource input to effects created by the outputs (or results) (see Figure).

Intentional Diversity Transformation

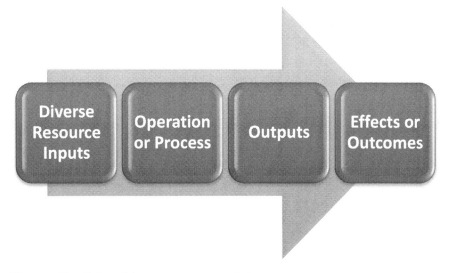

Figure: Traditional input-output model.

Effect means the action of one thing on another or some kind of outcome. A higher reported profit, reduced turnover of people of color, improved brand image, or reduced cycle time are examples outcomes or effects. Several of these effects will in turn influence the organization's future operations, thus becoming another input for the operation of a subsequent period. This relationship is clearest in the case of internal outcomes: New Diversity learning regarding multicultural marketing leads to improved marketing processes and techniques, which leads to a greater volume of customers from multicultural markets.

Intentional Diversity Transformation

In general, it is better to measure at the right of the above figure. Only when we see the effects do we know whether an intelligently planned use of diverse resource inputs and/or a well-managed operation was actually successful. There are also reasons to manage measures at the left of the figure. Sometimes these act as surrogate measures of conditions closer to the actual effects. For example, we might believe that our new multiethnic customers will be loyal, but we do not know that for sure. We may believe that rapid delivery means satisfied customers, but we do not know the exact nature of the relationship, or at least we would need a certain period of observation to learn how the two are connected. Because of this relationship, we may refer to the measures on the left of the figure as performance drivers. By understanding them, and taking care to manage them well, we can improve performance in a way that over time will result in better outcomes and effects (Olve, Roy, Wetter, 2000).

Good scorecards will combine outcome measures, of which profits is one, with performance drivers. Often it is difficult to draw the line between the two. They are interrelated in a chain of ends and means; for people in charge of logistics, delivery time is an outcome, but for purposes of customer relations, it may be considered as one of several performance drivers that can improve customer loyalty.

Intentional Diversity Transformation

What is important is that we measure thoroughly enough and use a credible Diversity measurement process to identify the specific measures that highlight diversity links to bottom-line organizational performance.

Building a Solid Diversity Measurement Strategy

A Diversity measurement process is not an end in itself. It has value only if the result it produces provides meaningful input into subsequent decisions you want to make and/or contributes to a more effective analysis of the organization's performance. Therefore, as you think about the choice and form of a particular measure stop and think carefully about what you would do with the results. Imagine receiving your first report summarizing this measure. What key decisions will these results tell you that you need to consider? Will another manager or executive, particularly one outside of the Diversity organization, consider recommendations based on this measure to be persuasive? Would these results provide a compelling foundation for a resource-allocation decision in your organization? Answers to questions such as these will help you formulate a solid diversity measurement strategy built with metrics that matter. Ideally, you will develop a measurement system that lets you answer questions such as, how much will we have to change "x" in order to achieve our target change in "y"? For example, if you increase the level of Diversity leadership competency in the first-level managers by 25 percent, how much will that change employee satisfaction scores that we know are linked to improved customer retention and sales? Or, if you reduce turnover among key technical staff in research and development (R&D) using improved sourcing techniques with key demographic groups by 10 percent, how long before that action begins to improve the new-product-development cycle time? A measurement system that can provide this kind of specificity is not easy to develop and may be beyond the reach of some organizations, but Diversity measurement quality is a continuum, not an absolute. As with most decisions, developing a strategic Diversity measurement system involves tradeoffs. To make the correct tradeoff, you need to choose the point along the measurement-quality continuum that you think your organization can reasonably achieve, yet not compromise the measurement system's integrity and credibility by selecting easy measures that have no real performance and value impact.

Even if you are unable to link new-product-cycle time reduction to customer satisfaction, and ultimately profitability, establishing just the first few links shown in Figure 2-3 between Diversity and the

Intentional Diversity Transformation

R&D cycle time would say a lot about Diversity's strategic influence.

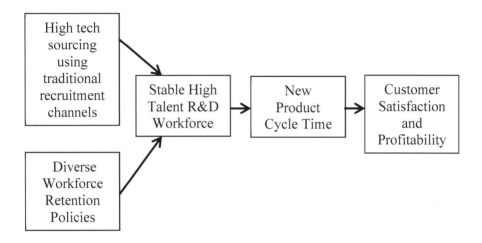

Figure: Links between Diversity and R&D cycle time.

By establishing the first few links shown, Diversity professionals could begin to talk about Diversity deliverables that make the difference in the organization's business.

Thinking strategically about measurement means understanding whether the measurement system you are building will provide you with the kinds of information that will help you manage the Diversity function in a strategic fashion. Understanding the value-creation process and developing construct-valid measures of that process form a top-down approach. A Diversity measurement system that only utilizes available measures without analyzing their performance and value-creation impact is a bottom-up approach that will be a waste of time in most cases. Ultimately, these bottom-up measures can undermine Diversity's strategic capability. To be effective, a strategic Diversity measurement approach is rooted in a process that links a clear line of sight to the organization's goals, objectives, and performance drivers.

Final Thoughts

This chapter has briefly outlined some of the issues in measurement and described some of the challenges that must be addressed to be effective. In the next series of chapters, the Diversity Return-on-Investment (DROI®) process and the application of measurement are explored to help you move beyond the limits of best available measurement approaches. It is designed to help you demonstrate Diversity's link to performance and bottom-line results in financial terms that highlight Diversity's value.

References

Becker, Brian E., Mark A. Huselid, and Dave Ulrich. *The HR Scorecard: Linking People, Strategy, and Performance*. Boston: Harvard Business School Press, 2001.

Fitz-enz, Jac. *How To Measure Human Resources Management*, 2nd ed. New York: McGraw-Hill, 1995.

Fitz-enz, Jac. *How To Measure Human Resources Management*. New York: McGraw-Hill, 1984.

Olve, Nils-Goran, Jan Roy, and Magnus Wetter. *Performance Drivers: A Practical Guide to Using the Balanced Scorecard*. Chichester, UK: John Wiley & Sons, 2000.

Part II

The Diversity Return on Investment (DROI®) Process and Transformational Analytics®

Chapter Four: Introduction to the Diversity ROI Process

Introduction

Measuring the results of Diversity initiatives will become a key strategic requirement to demonstrate its contribution to organizational goals and objectives. Diversity professionals and managers know they must begin to show how diversity is linked to the bottom-line in hard numbers. In short, they must calculate and report their ***diversity return-on-investment***. To get off to a good start, let's begin our journey by defining what we mean when we use the term "diversity".

What do we mean when we say "Diversity"?

When I use the term "*Diversity*", I define it as a collective mixture characterized by differences and similarities that are applied in pursuit of organizational objectives (Thomas, 1999). I define

Intentional Diversity Transformation

"Diversity Management" as the process of planning for, organizing, directing, and supporting these collective mixtures in a way that adds a measurable difference to organizational performance (Hubbard, 1999).

Diversity and its mixtures can be organized into four interdependent and sometimes overlapping aspects: Workforce Diversity, Behavioral Diversity, Structural Diversity, and Business Diversity.

Workforce Diversity encompasses group and situational identities of the organization's employees (i.e., gender, race, ethnicity, religion, sexual orientation, physical ability, age, family status, economic background and status, and geographical background and status). It also includes changes in the labor market demographics.

Behavioral Diversity encompasses work styles, thinking styles, learning styles, communication styles, aspirations, beliefs/value system as well as changes in the attitudes and expectation on the part of employees.

Structural Diversity encompasses interactions across functions, across organizational levels in the hierarchy, across divisions and between parent companies and subsidiaries, across organizations engaged in strategic alliances and cooperative ventures. As

Intentional Diversity Transformation

organizations attempt to become more flexible, less layered, more team-based, and more multi- and cross-functional, measuring this type of diversity will require more attention.

Business Diversity encompasses the expansion and segmentation of customer markets, the diversification of products and services offered, and the variety of operating environments in which organizations work and compete (i.e., legal and regulatory context, labor market realities, community and societal expectations/relationships, business cultures and norms). Increasing competitive pressures, globalization, rapid advances in product technologies, changing demographics in the customer bases both within domestic markets and across borders, and shifts in business/government relationships all signal a need to measure an organization's response and impact on business diversity.

What sites must be visited along the measurement journey?

Calculating diversity's return-on-investment requires asking key questions and performing key tasks along the way. To achieve a successful result, measuring diversity return-on-investment (DROI) requires a systematic approach that takes into account both costs and benefits. The Hubbard Diversity ROI Analysis Model provides a

Intentional Diversity Transformation

step-by-step approach that keeps the process manageable so users can tackle one issue at a time.

Hubbard Diversity ROI Analysis Model

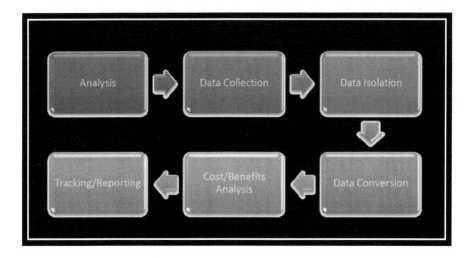

The model also emphasizes that this is a logical, systematic process, which flows from one step to another. Applying the model provides consistency from one DROI calculation to another. In essence, it suggests that the major aspects of diversity measurement you need to address include:

Analysis
- Knowing what you want to know

Intentional Diversity Transformation

Data Collection
- Collecting data and analyzing it

Data Isolation
- Isolating diversity's contribution

Data Conversion
- Converting the contribution to money

Cost/Benefits Analysis
- Calculating the costs and benefits

Tracking/Reporting
- Reporting it to others
- Tracking and assessing progress

Analysis

Step 1: Know What You Want To Know

Conducting a Diversity Return-on-Investment (DROI®) study requires that you clearly identify what you want to know as a result of implementing the study. This should be based upon, at bare

Intentional Diversity Transformation

minimum, the identification of a business problem or opportunity related to the organization's key business strategy. Second, you should be prepared to list a series of research questions you would like answered or hypotheses you would like to test. These questions may include things such as "In what racial categories do we have the most turnover?", "What diverse customer markets are not utilizing our products or services?", "How can we improve the idea and solution generation (creative) process using current cross-functional teams to improve operational performance?" etc.

While planning ways to address these research questions and ideas, it may be helpful to *begin with the end in mind*. That is, think of what will appear on your research report, create placeholders for them, and then generate the questions or hypotheses that must be answered in order for data to show up on the report as results. The final step in this phase is to summarize the questions you would like answered and formulate diversity measurement study objectives that will guide your work. Once this is done, you are ready to consider the appropriate data collection methods and develop your data collection plan.

Data Collection

Step 2: Collect Data and Analyze It

Data collection is central to the diversity return-on-investment (DROI) process. In some situations, post-DROI study data are collected and compared to pre-study situations, control group differences, and expectations. Both hard data, representing output, quality, cost, time and frequency; and soft data, including work habits, work climate, and attitudes are collected. Data are collected using a variety of methods including but not limited to:

- Follow-up surveys
- Post-study interviews
- Focus groups
- Short term pilot project assignments
- Action plans
- Performance contracts (agreements to produce certain levels of results)
- Performance monitoring (reports and other literature reviews)
- Etc.

The important challenge in the data collection phase is to select the method or methods appropriate for the organizational setting and within the time and budget constraints of the organization. During this phase, you will identify the data collection processes and specific metrics to use, create the appropriate evaluation instruments, and apply an organizational change methodology such as the Hubbard Diversity 9-S Framework (Shared Vision, Shared Values, Standards, Strategy, Structure, Systems, Style, Skills and Staff).

Data Isolation

Step 3: Isolate Diversity's Contribution

An often-overlooked issue in most diversity assessments or evaluation studies is the process of isolating the effects of diversity. In this step of the process, specific strategies are explored, which determine the amount of output performance directly related to the diversity initiative. This step is essential because there are many factors that will influence performance data after the diversity initiative. The result is increased accuracy and credibility of the DROI® calculation. The following strategies have been utilized by organizations to tackle this important issue:

- Control groups
- Trend lines (Time Series Analysis)
- Forecasting model
- Participant estimates

Intentional Diversity Transformation

- Supervisor of participant estimates
- Senior management estimates
- Expert estimates
- Subordinate's estimates (those who work for the participants)
- Identifying other influencing factors
- Customer inputs

Collectively, these strategies provide a comprehensive set of tools to tackle the important and critical issue of isolating the effects of diversity initiatives.

Calculating and isolating Diversity's return-on-investment will require an analysis of operational and other business processes to isolate the specific areas where Diversity can be applied to improve business performance. One tool to analyze operational processes is the "S-I-P-O-C Chain". This analysis tool allows you to break down operational processes and view them in terms of the way business is done from *Supplier* to *Input* to *Process* to *Output* to *Customer*. Once all contributing factors have been identified and their contributions calculated you would be ready to convert the contribution to money.

Intentional Diversity Transformation

Data Conversion

Step 4: Convert the Contribution to Money

To calculate the Diversity return-on-investment, data collected in a DROI® evaluation study are converted to monetary values and are compared to the Diversity initiative costs. This requires a value to be placed on each unit of data connected with the initiative. There are at least ten different strategies available to convert data to monetary values. The specific strategy selected usually depends on the type of data and the initiative under analysis:

- **Output data** are converted to profit contribution or cost saving. In this strategy, output increases are converted to monetary value based on their unit contribution to profit or the unit of cost reduction.
- The **cost of quality** is calculated and quality improvements are directly converted to cost savings.
- For Diversity initiatives where employee time is saved, the **participant's wages and benefits** are used for the value of time. Because a variety of programs focus on improving the time required to complete projects, processes, or daily activities, the value of time becomes an important and critical issue.
- **Historical costs** are used when they are available for a specific variable. In this case, organizational cost data are utilized to establish the specific value of an improvement.

Intentional Diversity Transformation

- When available, **internal and external experts** may be used to estimate a value for an improvement. In this situation, the credibility of the estimate hinges on the expertise and reputation of the individual.

- **External databases** are sometimes available to estimate the value or cost of data items. Research, government, and industry databases can provide important information for these values. The difficulty lies in finding a specific database related to the diversity initiative under analysis.

- **Participants** estimate the value of the data item. For this approach to be effective, participants must be capable of providing a value for the improvement.

- **Supervisors of participants** provide estimates when they are both willing and capable of assigning values to the improvement. This approach is especially useful when participants are not fully capable of providing this input or in situations where supervisors need to confirm or adjust the participant's estimate.

- **Senior management** may provide estimates on the values of an improvement. This approach is particularly helpful to establish values for performance measures that are very important to senior management.

Intentional Diversity Transformation

- **Diversity staff** estimates may be used to determine a value of an output data item. In these cases, it is essential for the estimates to be provided on an unbiased basis.

Step 4 in the Hubbard Diversity Return-on-investment (DROI®) Analysis Model is very important and is absolutely necessary for determining the monetary benefits from a diversity initiative. The process is challenging, particularly with soft data, but can be methodologically accomplished using one or more of these strategies.

Cost/Benefits Analysis

Step 5: Calculate the Costs and Benefits

Calculating the Diversity Initiative Costs

To successfully calculate DROI, both cost and benefits must be tracked and calculated in the process. The first part of the equation on a cost/benefit analysis is the Diversity initiative costs. Tabulating the costs involves monitoring or developing all of the related costs of the diversity initiative targeted for the DROI® calculation. Among the cost components that should be included are:

Intentional Diversity Transformation

- The cost to design and develop the Diversity initiative, possibly prorated over the expected life of the initiative;
- The cost of any materials and external staff resources utilized;
- The costs of any facilities, travel, lodging, etc.
- Salaries, plus employee benefits of the employee's involved;
- Administrative and overhead costs allocated in some way.

Calculating the Diversity Return on Investment

The diversity return-on-investment is calculated using the initiative's benefits and costs. The benefit/cost ratio (BCR) is the initiative benefits divided by cost. In formula form it is:

BCR = Diversity Initiative Benefits / Diversity Initiative Costs

Sometimes the ratio is stated as a cost-to-benefit ratio, although the formula is the same as BCR.

The Diversity return on investment calculation uses the net benefits of the diversity initiative divided by the initiative costs. The net benefits are the Diversity initiative benefits minus the costs. As a formula, it is stated as:

DROI% = (Net Diversity Initiative Benefits / Initiative Costs)*100

Intentional Diversity Transformation

In other words, the DROI formula is calculated as:

$$\frac{\text{Diversity Benefits} - \text{Initiative Costs}}{\text{Initiative Cost}} \times 100$$

This is the same basic formula used in evaluating other investments where the ROI is traditionally reported as earnings divided by investment. The DROI® from some Diversity initiatives is often high. DROI® figures above 450% are not uncommon.

Identifying Intangible Benefits

In addition to tangible, monetary benefits, most Diversity initiatives will have intangible, non-monetary benefits. The DROI® calculation is based on converting both hard and soft data to monetary values. Intangible benefits include items such as:

- Increased job satisfaction
- Increased organizational commitment
- Improved teamwork
- Reduced conflict
- Etc.

During data analysis, every attempt is made to convert all data to monetary values. All hard data such as output, quality, and time are converted to monetary values. The conversion of soft data is attempted for each data item. However, if the process used for conversion is too subjective or inaccurate, the resulting values can lose credibility in the process. This data should be listed as an intangible benefit with the appropriate explanation. For some diversity initiatives, intangible, non-monetary benefits are extremely valuable, often carrying as much influence as the hard data items.

Tracking/Reporting

Step 6: Report It to Others

Next, it is critical that you have an organized communications plan to let others know the progress and challenges being addressed by diversity initiatives. During the development cycle of the communications plan, it is important to identify communication vehicles to use, how and when the report will be created, when it will be delivered and how to evaluate its implementation.

Intentional Diversity Transformation

Step 7: Track and Assess Progress

Finally, in order to maintain any gains made or benefits from lessons learned during the process, you must make plans to track and assess the effectiveness of your diversity initiatives over time.

Your Challenge

In summary, the implementation of your Diversity return-on-investment DROI® study is very critical to the success of the organization and the credibility and survival of the Diversity profession. In order to be taken seriously, Diversity organizations must become adept at measuring Diversity results that tie diversity to the organization's bottom-line objectives. By using a systematic, logical, planned approach, the Diversity return-on-investment DROI® process is one of the organization's best investments in improved performance!

Now that you have an idea of what previous Diversity scorecards contained and the Diversity ROI process which supported them, you are ready to learn how to construct a new type of framework and analytics into a Logic Model called: Diversity Transformational Analytics®. This approach will help further refine and evolve your Diversity Scorecard into a Diversity ROI-based DROI® system which provides the ability to more accurately and consistently reach the organization's "strategic Diversity future-state" level of outcomes and impact.

References

Hubbard, Edward E. *Diversity Return on Investment (DROI®) Fundamentals: Ensuring Diversity Initiatives Demonstrate ROI Impact Value on the Bottom-line.* Petaluma, CA: Global Insights Publishing, 2014.

Chapter Five: Introduction to Diversity Transformational Analytics

Can Diversity & Inclusion Really Affect the Bottom-line with Predictive Transformational Impact?

The primary issue that Diversity must deal with is very hard for some to imagine and believe, that is, showing Diversity's measurable impact on organizational strategy and the financial bottom-line. The ability to utilize a diverse mix of human and other resources to create a unique blend of strategy-focused solutions, by its very nature, creates an innovative competitive process that is difficult to copy – thus making it a competitive advantage (largely invisible to competitors). This notion is covered in detail in my books: "How to Calculate Diversity Return on Investment" and "Diversity Business Alignment Maps: Utilizing Intangible Human Capital Assets to Produce Tangible Business Results".

Intentional Diversity Transformation

What's Next?

Although most organizations have come a long way in introducing better metrics for Diversity on their corporate scorecards, there is still a great deal of work to be done. Even the best scorecards need improvement in some key areas to evolve to the next level of performance impact. Metrics in several Diversity Scorecards currently focus on "counting activities or outputs" which are "transactional" in nature (such as employee representation metrics by race, rank and gender). They **do not** produce "intentional outcomes" and "organizational transformations".

There is a distinct difference between generating "outputs" from scorecard action plans and producing "Strategic Outcomes" and "Intended Transformational Impacts". I define "Strategic Outcomes" and "Intended Transformational Impacts as "planned, intended measurable results or effects of an action, situation, or event; something that follows due to a planned execution of measurable actions which result in a specific intended *consequence (or unintended consequences)* that add value and drive measurable, sustainable change.

Intentional Diversity Transformation

Evolving the Diversity Scorecard's Business Impact

Current Diversity Scorecards must evolve to move beyond simply counting heads and reporting out "representation-based metrics and analytics only. They must elevate their utility to a level that utilizes "Logic Model-based predictive analytics and processes which more accurately generate "Strategic Outcomes" and "Intended Transformational Impacts.

What are Analytics

Analytics come in different types with a specific focus. They can be defined as follows:

- **"Analytics"** is the Science of Analysis
- **"Descriptive Analytics"** tells what has happened in the past and usually the cause of the outcome.
- **"Predictive Analytics"** focuses on the future telling what is likely to happen given a stated approach.
- **"Prescriptive Analytics"** tells us what is the 'Best' course of action.

Descriptive Diversity Analytics can help us understand human capital challenges and opportunities in utilizing a diverse workforce.

Intentional Diversity Transformation

Whereas Predictive Diversity Analytics, helps us identify investment value and a means to improve future outcomes from Diversity interventions and initiatives. Prescriptive Analytics suggest what actions we need to take that are in alignment with best practices which have proven to work in real life.

Combined with Logic Models, this approach creates a strategic set of actionable plans, strategies, or maps with clear outcomes and explicit steps for solving Diversity problems and issues.

Intentional Diversity Transformation

A basic logic model (Figure 1) typically has two "sides"—process and outcome. The process section describes the program's inputs (resources), activities, and outputs (direct products). The outcome section describes the intended effects of the program, which can be short term, intermediate, and/or long term. Assumptions under which the program or intervention operates, and the contextual factors can also be included in a logic model. They are often noted in a box below or on the left side of the logic model diagram. Figure 1, below, illustrates the components of a logic model.

Figure 1. Layout of a General Logic Model

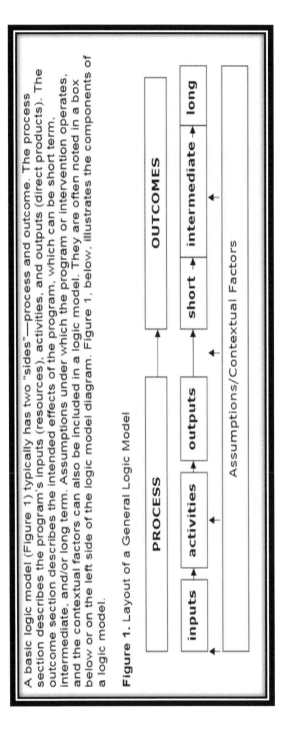

Source: Department of Health and Human Services, Centers for Disease Control and Prevention, National Center for Chronic Disease Prevention and Health Promotion Evaluation Guide

Intentional Diversity Transformation

Logic models are used in a wide variety of applications to drive specific results and outcomes. Here are a few examples:

Basic Logic Model

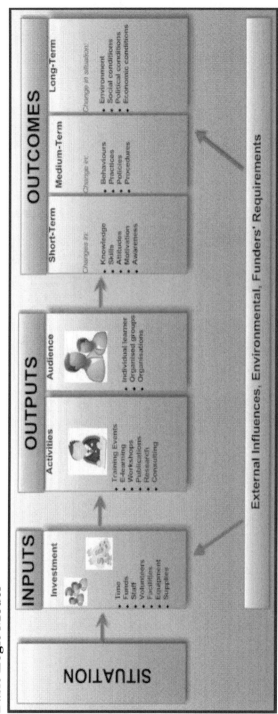

Intentional Diversity Transformation

This Logic Model highlights the basic elements which are contained in a Logic modelling process to affect an environment, social conditions, political conditions, and economic conditions. In addition the model reflects the points where external influences, environmental, and funder requirements will impact the process.

Intentional Diversity Transformation

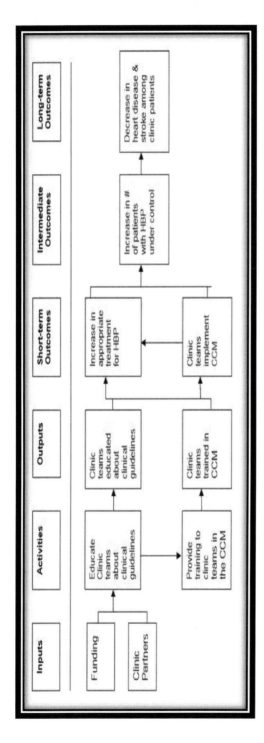

This Logic Model displays the CDC Chronic Care Model (CCM) Process for High Blood Pressure and Heart Disease & Stroke Prevention. It details the expected evidence-based outcomes that will result by operationalizing the Chronic Care Model elements using trained diverse work teams.

Intentional Diversity Transformation

Logic Model to Build Strong Families

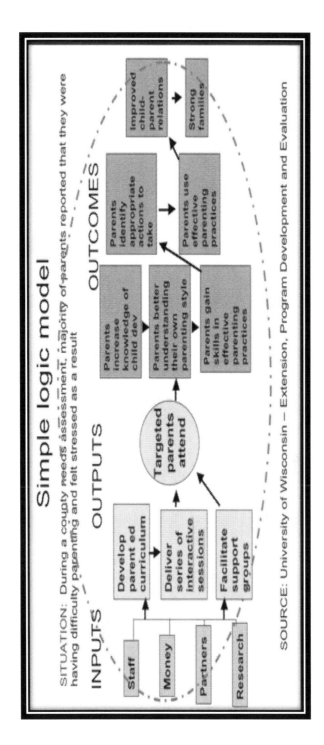

Intentional Diversity Transformation

This Logic Model highlights an application which focuses on building strong families. It details the expected evidence-based outcomes (such as increasing parental knowledge of child development, enhancing parental choices regarding the appropriate actions to take to generate effective child-parent relations which ultimately produce strong families) by operationalizing the model elements.

Intentional Diversity Transformation

Logic Model for Program Development

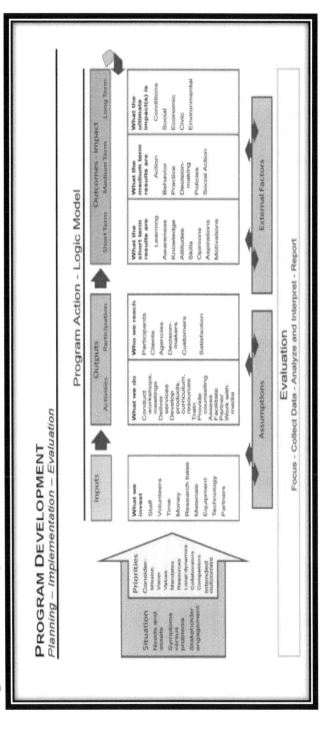

Intentional Diversity Transformation

This Logic Model reflects the major Logic Model elements in building an effective program. It details the expected evidence-based outcomes that will result by operationalizing the model elements and the requirements for evaluating the process.

Intentional Diversity Transformation

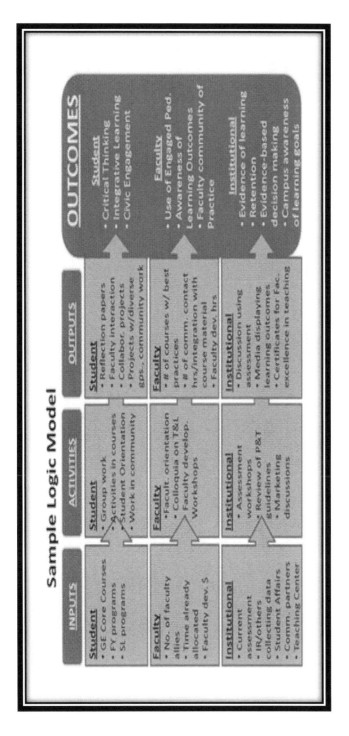

Intentional Diversity Transformation

Higher Education Focused Logic Model

This Logic Model highlights an application which focuses on building a comprehensive engagement strategy for Students, Faculty and the institution's goal to generate results for each audience on campus. It details the expected evidence-based outcomes that will result by operationalizing the model elements.

Logic models are tools for planning, describing, managing, communicating, and evaluating a program or intervention. They graphically represent the relationships between a program's activities and its intended effects, state the assumptions that underlie expectations that a program will work, and frame the context in which the program operates. Logic models are not static documents. In fact they should be revised periodically to reflect new evidence, lessons learned, and changes in context, resources, activities, or expectations. Logic models increase the likelihood that a Diversity and Inclusion intervention effort will be successful because they:

- Communicate the purpose of the program and expected results.
- Describe the actions expected to lead to the desired results.
- Become a reference point for everyone involved in the program.

Intentional Diversity Transformation

- Improve program staff expertise in planning, implementation, and evaluation.
- Involve stakeholders, enhancing the likelihood of resource commitment.
- Incorporate findings from other research and ROI-based initiatives.
- Identify potential obstacles to program operation so that staff can address them early on.

Intentional Diversity Transformation

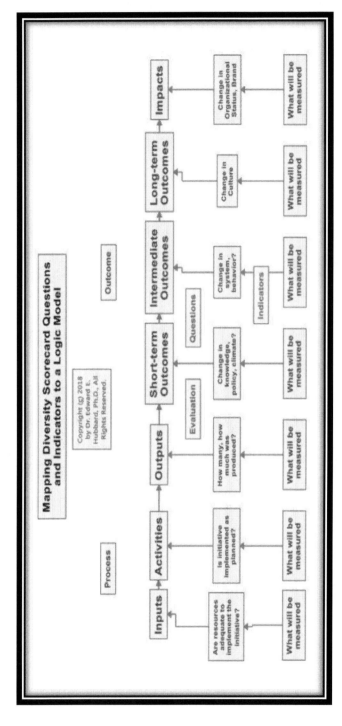

Mapping Diversity Scorecard Questions and Indicators to a Logic Model

Intentional Diversity Transformation

Evolving the Diversity Scorecard requires that we ask key strategic measurement questions and perform specific actions along the Logic Model path to create transformational outcomes, impact and change. This is not a generic, random process. It involves possessing specific Transformational Analytics knowledge, skills and competencies to correctly drive each outcome phase (Initial, Intermediate, and Long-term) to achieve the desired change effect and impact. To gain the tremendous benefits that Diversity and Inclusion offers, our Scorecards and other measurement tools must take full advantage of "next level" practices such as the Hubbard Diversity Measurement Sciences and Analytics® to ensure better predictive accuracy to deliver strategic Diversity outcomes and transformational impacts. As Diversity practitioners, our utility, organizational value, brand reputation, and success will depend on it.

As mentioned earlier, there is a distinct difference between generating "outputs" from scorecard action plans and producing "Strategic Outcomes" and "Intended Transformational Impacts". I define "Strategic Outcomes" and "Intended Transformational Impacts as "planned, intended measurable results or effects of an action, situation, or event; something that follows due to a planned execution of measurable actions which result in a specific intended *consequence (or unintended consequences)* that add value and drive measurable, sustainable change. The use of "Logic Models" helps

Intentional Diversity Transformation

to demonstrate this process and can show the resulting evidence-based outcomes that are produced when this type of strategic systems modelling is utilized.

Diversity Transformational Analytics® offer a new point of departure due to their use as part of a planned execution of measurable actions which will result in a specific intended *consequence (or unintended consequences)* that add value and drives measurable, sustainable change. When we map Diversity Scorecard questions and indicators to a Logic Model, we will need key metrics to evaluate our success at each stage in the process. A Sample of the Logic Model categories and metrics might include the following:

Intentional Diversity Transformation

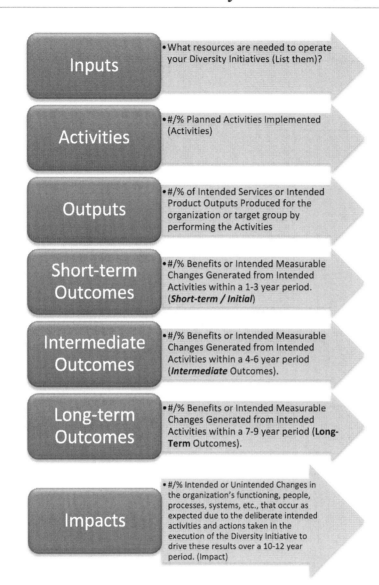

Sample metrics and analytics to support each stage might include the following:

Intentional Diversity Transformation

Inputs
- # of People Resources
- $ Invested
- Types of Research Utilized
- # of Collaborations
- # of Facilities Used
- #/Types of Equipment Utilized
- #/% Products/Materials Used

Activities
- #/% Specific Tasks Identified
- #/% New Training Programs in Development
- #/% Operations Processes being Implemented
- #/% People Currently in Training

Intentional Diversity Transformation

Outputs
- #/% People Trained
- #/% Services Delivered
- #/% Meetings Held
- #/% Workshops Delivered
- # New Product/Services Developed
- #/% Increase in New Customer Referrals

Short-term Outcomes
- $ Costs Reduced
- # New Innovative Products Developed that Generate Over $100K
- % Increase in Employee Satisfaction
- #/% Increase in Employee Awareness, Knowledge, Skills, Attitudes
- % Increase in Employee Engagement

Intentional Diversity Transformation

Intermediate Outcomes
- Increased $ Revenues Generated from New Customers
- #/% New Lines of Business Created from Innovateive Products and Services
- #/% Reduction in Employee Turnover Costs
- Imcreased Brand Image Scores
- #/% Effective Use of Practices Taught

Long-term Outcomes
- $ Increase in Shareholder Value
- #/% Resolution of Community-based Issues/Problems
- Increased Perceptions regarding Overall Employment Brand (% Favorable Response)
- #/% New Behaviors Integrated into Culture & Systems

Intentional Diversity Transformation

- #/% Intended or Unintended Changes in the organization's functioning, people, processes, systems, etc., that occur as expected due to the deliberate intended activities and actions taken in the execution of the Diversity Initiative to drive these results over a 10-12 year period. (Impact)

Organizational Transformation and Change

In order to provide a model of organizational performance and change, at least two lines of theorizing need to be explored- "organizational functioning" and "organizational change". I would like to go beyond mere description and suggest causal linkages that hypothesize how strategic performance is affected and how effective, "intentional" change occurs. Change is depicted in terms of both process and content, with particular emphasis on transformational as compared with transactional factors. Transformational change occurs as a response to the external environment and directly affects organizational mission and strategy, the organizations leadership, and culture. In tum, the transactional factors are affected-structure, systems, management practices, and climate. These transformational and transactional factors together affect motivation, which, in tum, affects performance. In support of the model's potential validity, theory and research as well as practice will be highlighted in this section to lay the foundation for the use of Transformational Analytics and Logic Models to drive organizational performance outcomes.

Organization change is a kind of chaos (Gleick, 1987). The number of variables changing at the same time, the magnitude of environmental change, and the frequent resistance of human systems create a whole union of processes that are extremely difficult to predict and almost impossible to control. Nevertheless, there are consistent patterns that exist-linkages among classes of events that have been demonstrated repeatedly in the research literature and can be seen in actual organizations. The enormous and pervasive impact of culture and beliefs to the point where it causes organizations to do fundamentally unsound things from a business point of view-would be an example.

To build a *most likely* model describing the causes of organizational performance and change, we must explore two important lines of thinking. First, we must understand more thoroughly how organizations function (i.e., what leads to what). Second, using the Burke-Litwin model of causation (1992), we can understand how organizations might be deliberately changed. The purpose of this section is to lay out an explanation. More specifically, it will present a framework for understanding a causal model of organizational performance and change. But, first, a bit of background.

In our organizational consulting work, we try very hard to link the practice to sound theory and research. The linkage typically is in the direction of theory and research to practice: that is, to ground our consultation in what is known, what is theoretically and empirically sound and is verified with metrics and analytics. Thus, any of our organizational models would stem from an input-throughput-output-outcome continuum, with a feedback loop, format. The models presented in this book are definitely of that genre. In other words, the fundamental framework for the models are evolved from theory and validated with science and research. The components of the model and what causes what and in what order, on the other hand, have evolved from our practice using this scientific foundation.

Intentional Diversity Transformation

Origins of Transformational and Transactional Dynamics

To fully appreciate the need for an evolved Diversity and Inclusion Scorecard that generates specific, intended outcomes, we must better understand the complexity and requirements for driving behavioral performance and strategic change in the organization. This complexity and its requirements is rooted in the earliest notions of climate, culture and strategy and the need to respond to external environmental demands.

The concept of transformational change in organizations is suggested in the writings of such people as Bass (1985), Burke (1986), Bums (1978), McClelland (1975), and Tichy and Devanna (1986). The figure below contains a display of the transformational variables. By *transformational* these researchers meant areas in which alteration is likely caused by interaction with environmental forces (both within and without) and will require entirely new sets of behavior from organizational members.

A Model of Organizational Performance and Change:

The TRANSFORMATIONAL Factors

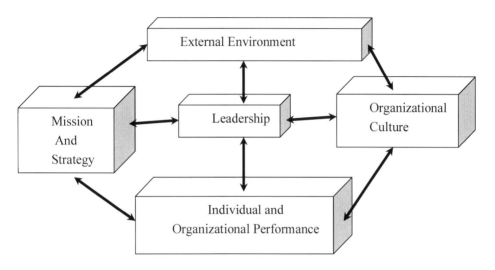

It is true, of course, that members can influence their organization's environment so that certain changes are minimized (e.g., lobbying activities, forming or being involved in trade associations and coalitions). The feedback loop shown in the model is meant to reflect this kind of influence. The point here is that for the most part organizational change is initiated by forces from the organization's external environment (e.g., changes in the competitive environment, government regulations, and technological breakthroughs). Not everyone agreed with the early researchers premise. Torbert (1989), for example, argues that organizational transformation emanates from transformational leaders, not from the environment. Burke and others agreed that strong leaders make a difference, especially in the early stages of their tenure. However, they wrote that these leaders would be responding to forces in their organization's environment. This leader responsiveness does not mean passivity. Astute leaders are people who scan their organization's external environment, choose the forces they wish to deal with, and take action accordingly. This leadership process is neither passive nor done in isolation.

The figure which follows contains the transactional variables. These variables are very similar to those originally isolated earlier by Litwin and, in part (structural effects on climate), later by Michela et al. (1988). By transactional, the researchers meant that the primary way of alteration is via relatively short-term reciprocity among people and groups. In other words, "You do this for me and I'll do that for you." This transformational-transactional way of thinking about organizations they were using for the model, as noted earlier, comes from theory about leadership.

Intentional Diversity Transformation

The distinction has been characterized as differences between a leader and a manager. Burke (1986) combined both the theorizing of Zaleznik (1977) and Burns (1978) to clarify further these distinctions and to hypothesize how each type, leader or manager, could empower others effectively. With respect to the model, and in keeping with the leader (transformational) versus manager (transactional) distinctions, transformational change is therefore associated more with leadership, whereas transactional change is more within the purview of management.

Intentional Diversity Transformation

A Model of Organizational Performance and Change:

The TRANSACTIONAL Factors

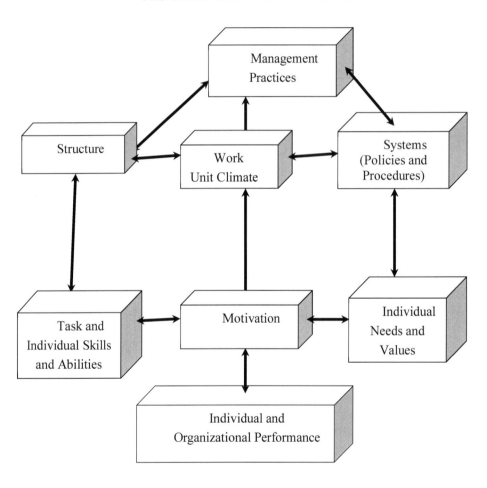

Intentional Diversity Transformation

With this broad distinction of transformational versus transactional in mind, we can now proceed with a more specific explanation of the model. And, at the risk of erring on the side of brevity, the next section defines each category or box in the model. With each box definition there is at least one reference from the literature that helps to clarify further what is meant by these descriptions.

External environment is any outside condition or situation that influences the performance of the organization (e.g., marketplaces, world financial conditions, political/governmental circumstances). For a broad view of the changing nature of our world economy, see Drucker (1986). For a more specific perspective on how the external environment affects the organization, see Pfeffer and Salancik (1978).

Mission and strategy is what the organization's (a) top management believes is and has declared is the organization's mission and strategy and (b) what employees believe is the central purpose of the organization. Apparently, the mere fact of having a written mission statement is important to organizational effectiveness (Pearce & David, 1987). Strategy is how the organization intends to achieve that purpose over an extended time scale.

Intentional Diversity Transformation

Leadership is executives providing overall organizational direction and serving as behavioral role models for all employees. When assessing this category we would include followers' perceptions of executive practices and values. As our model shows, we make a distinction between leadership and management. This difference follows the thinking of Bennis and Nanus (1985), Burke (1986), Bums (1978), and Zaleznik (1977).

Culture is "the way we do things around here." This clear, simple definition comes from Deal and Kennedy (1982). To be a bit more comprehensive in our definition, I should add that culture is the collection of overt and covert rules, values, and principles that are enduring and guide organizational behavior. Understanding an organization's history, especially the values and customs of the founder(s), is key to explaining culture (Schein, 1983). Also, as stated earlier, culture provides a "meaning system" for organizational members.

Structure includes the arrangement of functions and people into specific areas and levels of responsibility, decision-making authority, communication, and relationships to assure effective implementation of the organization's mission and strategy. Perhaps the classic articles on structure and no doubt some of the ones cited

Intentional Diversity Transformation

most often are by Duncan (1979) and Galbraith (1974). For perspectives about organizational structure and the future, see Jelinek, Litterer, and Miles (1986) and Peters (1988).

Management practices are what managers do in the normal course of events to use the human and material resources at their disposal to carry out the organization's strategy. By practices I mean a particular cluster of specific behaviors. An example of a behavioral management practice is "encouraging subordinates to initiate innovative approaches to tasks and projects." As a practice, two managers may "encourage subordinates" to the same extent, but how specifically each one does it may differ. This is suggested based upon the research of such people as Boyatzis (1982), Burke and Coruzzi (1987), and Luthans (1988).

Systems are standardized policies and mechanisms that facilitate work, primarily manifested in the organization's reward systems, management information systems **(MIS),** and in such control systems as performance appraisal, goal and budget development, and human resource allocation. This category of the model covers a lot of ground. Some references that help to explain what I mean by the subcategories include Lawler (1981) on reward systems, Keen (1981) on **MIS,** Flamholtz (1979) on control systems, and Schuler

Intentional Diversity Transformation

and Jackson (1987) with their linkage of human resource management systems and practices to strategy.

Climate is the collective current impressions, expectations, and feelings that members of local work units have that, in turn, affect their relations with their boss, with one another, and with other units. For further clarification of what is meant by climate, see James and Jones (1974), Litwin, Humphrey, and Wilson (1978), and Michela et al. (1988).

Task requirements and individual skills/abilities are the required behavior for task effectiveness, including specific skills and knowledge required of people to accomplish the work for which they have been assigned and for which they feel directly responsible. Essentially, this box concerns what is often referred to as job-person match. This domain of the model represents mainstream industrial/organizational psychology. Almost any good textbook, such as Maier and Verser (1982), will provide thorough coverage of this category of the model. On the job side, see Campion and Thayer (1987) for an up-to-date analysis of job design, and for the person side, at the general manager level, Herbert and Deresky (1987) provide a useful perspective on matching a person's talents with business strategy.

Intentional Diversity Transformation

Individual needs and values are the specific psychological factors that provide desire and worth for individual actions or thoughts. Many behavioral scientists believe that enriched jobs enhance motivation and there is evidence to support this belief, yet as Hackman and Oldham (1980) have appropriately noted, not everyone has a desire for his or her job to be enriched. For some members of the workforce, their idea of enrichment concerns activities off the job, not on the job.

As the American workforce continues to become even more diverse, the ability to understand differences among people regarding their needs and values with respect to work and job satisfaction increases in importance. See, for example, Kravetz (1988) regarding changes in the workforce and Plummer (1989) on our changing values (i.e., more emphasis on self-actualization).

Motivation is aroused behavior tendencies to move toward goals, take needed action, and persist until satisfaction is attained. This is the net resultant motivation: that is, the resultant net energy generated by the sum of achievement, power, affection, discovery, and other important human motives. The article by Evans (1986) is especially relevant because his model for understanding motivation in the workplace is not only multifaceted but the facets are very similar to the model shared by Burke and others.

Individual and organizational performance is the outcome or result as well as the indicator of effort and achievement (e.g., productivity, customer satisfaction, profit, and quality). At the organizational level the work of Cameron, Whetten, and their colleagues is especially relevant to this box: see, for example, Cameron (1980), Cameron and Whetten (1982), and Cameron and Whetton (1981), and at the individual level the article by Latham, Cummings, and Mitchell (1981).

This foundational background sets the framework and science behind the next evolution I feel is required in the structure and design of an effective Diversity and Inclusion Scorecard. I created this new scorecard framework with the transformational factors in mind. I also realized that this new scorecard design must be both practical and strategic in nature to assist Diversity practitioners in creating transformational change. It is critical that this new scorecard is linked and aligned with the organization's key business goals, objectives and long-term outcomes. This elemental alignment helps drive measurable performance improvement to the bottom-line. In the next chapter, I will discuss and review the structure and use of this evolved Diversity and Inclusion Scorecard as well as highlight sample metrics and analytics that chronicle and drive a Diversity and Initiative's performance.

References

Bass, B.M. (1985). Leadership and performance beyond expectations. New York: Free Press. Bernstein, W.M., & Burke, W.W. (in press). Modeling organizational meaning systems. In R.W. Woodman and W.A. Pasmore (Eds.), Research in organizational change and development (Vol. 3). Greenwich, CT: JAi Press.

Burke, W.W., & Litwin, G.H. (1989). A causal model of organizational performance. InJ.W. Pfeiffer (Ed.), The 1989 annual: Developing human resources. San Diego, CA: University Associates.

Burke, W.W. (1986). Leadership as empowering others. In S. Srivastva and Associates, Executive

power: How executives influence people and organizations. San Francisco: Jossey-Bass.

Burns, J.M. (1978). Leadership. New York: Harper & Row.

Burns, T., & Stalker, G. (1961). The management of innovation. London: Tavistock.

Hackman, J.R., & Oldham, G.R. (1980). Work redesign. Reading, MA: Addison-Wesley.

Katz, D., & Kahn, R.L. (1978). The social psychology of organizations (2nd ed.). New York: John Wiley.

Lawrence, P.R., & Lorsch, J.W. (1969). Developing organizations: Diagnosis and action. Reading, MA: Addison-Wesley.

Litwin, G.H., & Stringer, R.A. (1968). Motivation and organizational climate. Boston, MA: Harvard Business School.

McClelland, D.C. (1975). Power: The inner experience. New York: Irvington.

Michela, J.L., Boni, S.M., Manderlink, G., Bernstein, W.M., O'Malley, M., Burke, W.W., & Schecter, C. (1988). Perceptions of the work environment vary with organization and group membership and organizational position of the group. Working Paper. Unpublished manuscript, Teachers College, Columbia University, New York.

Nadler, D.A., & Tushman, M.L. (1977). A diagnostic model for organization behavior. In J.R. Hackman, E.E. Lawler, & L.W. Porter (Eds.), Perspectives on behavior in organizations. New York: McGraw-Hill.

Schein, E.H. (1985). Organizational culture and leadership. San Francisco: Jossey-Bass.

Tagiuri, R., & Litwin, G.H. (Eds.). (1968). Organizational climate: Explorations of a concept. Cambridge,

MA: Harvard University Press.

Tichy, N.M., & Devanna, M.A. (1986). The transformational leader: Molding tomorrow's corporation

winners. New York: John Wiley.

Weisbord, M.R. (1976). Organizational diagnosis: Six places to look for trouble with or without a theory. Group & Organization Studies, 1, 430-447.

Chapter Six: The Transformational Diversity Scorecard

An Innovative Evolution in Diversity ROI Metrics Design that Drives Strategic Evidence-based Results and Impact!

In the Preface of my book "The Diversity Scorecard: Evaluating the Impact of Diversity on Organizational Performance (2004)", I mentioned that senior leaders and Diversity professionals are eager to see practical applications of the models, techniques, theories, strategies, and issues that constitute the Diversity arena. In recent years, Diversity practitioners have developed an intense desire to learn about Diversity measurement strategies that create compelling evidence which highlights how Diversity adds value to organizational performance and the bottom line.

In this book, you will be introduced to an innovative, evolutionary system in Diversity ROI metrics and analytics which allows you to drive each stage of your Diversity initiatives using "**Hubbard Logic**

Intentional Diversity Transformation

Model Sciences®". This process helps you generate "Strategic Outcomes" and "Intended Transformational Impacts. It will provide step-by-step Transformational Analytic processes that are proven to work in the real environment of the workplace.

In this book, I address the question: How can Diversity practitioners drive Diversity ROI-based initiatives that produce a specific intended outcome and guides their Diversity Equity and Inclusion (DEI) initiative execution strategy as well as business success and ROI.

What Is a Balanced Scorecard?

In my book "The Diversity Scorecard: Evaluating the Impact of Diversity on Organizational Performance (2004)", I discussed that a Balanced Diversity scorecard assists organizations in maximizing two key issues: (1) achieving effective Diversity and Inclusion performance, and (2) implementing a comprehensive Diversity strategy and measurement process.

Intentional Diversity Transformation

It is a carefully selected set of measures derived from an organization's strategy. The measures selected for the scorecard represent a tool for leaders to use when communicating with employees and external stakeholders regarding the outcomes and performance drivers by which the organization will achieve its mission and strategic objectives. A simple definition, however, cannot tell us everything about the balanced scorecard. In many organizations, and research into best practices of scorecard use, this tool serves at least three functions:

1. A measurement system
2. A strategic management system
3. A communication tool

The Balanced Scorecard as a Measurement System

In "The Diversity Scorecard" book, I also discussed the limiting features of financial performance measures. Although they provide an excellent review of what has happened in the past, they are inadequate in addressing the real value-creating mechanisms in today's organizations—the intangible assets such as knowledge, experiences, and networks of relationships. We might call financial measures *lag indicators.* They are outcomes of actions previously taken. The balanced scorecard complements these lag indicators with the drivers of future economic performance, or *lead indicators*. Where do these performance measures (both lag and lead) come from? The answer is the organization's strategy. All of the measures on the balanced scorecard serve as translations of the organization's strategy. Examine the Balanced Scorecard Figure shown on the next page (Kaplan and Norton, 1996).

Intentional Diversity Transformation

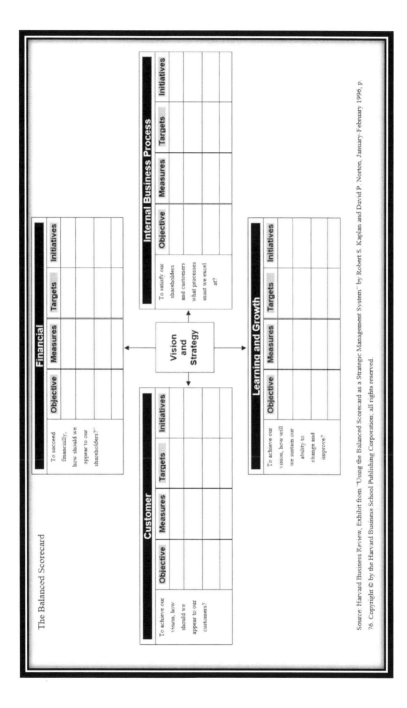

Intentional Diversity Transformation

The Diversity Scorecard was designed using a similar framework with Diversity Perspectives:

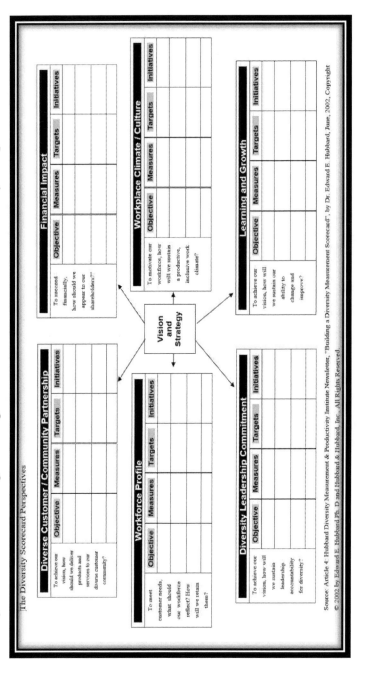

Intentional Diversity Transformation

The new Hubbard Intentional Diversity Transformation Scorecard® represent a new point of departure in Diversity measurement and analytics tracking. It is designed as a Strategic Outcomes Scorecard using Diversity Transformational Analytics® to drive organizational change and "next level" impacts (based upon a "Logic Model" framework). An example of this revolutionary design is shown below:

Intentional Diversity Transformation

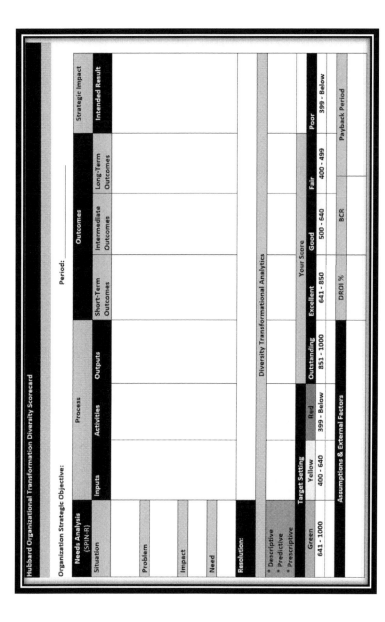

Page 208

Intentional Diversity Transformation

This scorecard is designed using the following Perspectives:

- **Needs Analysis** – this section allows you to describe the specific Situation, Problem, Impact, Need and Resolution which this Diversity Scorecard was designed to address. No matter what business or performer need you are trying to address, it is critical to conduct a Needs Analysis to establish a baseline for the problem or situation. It also serves as the "initial Gap Analysis" to identify the difference between "Ideally" what the organization desires and "Actually" what current state exists. The "Gap" becomes the work you do to transition the "Actual" to the "Ideal" state.

Intentional Diversity Transformation

Process – this section allows you to outline the process flow of the Diversity and Inclusion initiative detailing its Inputs, Activities, and Outputs. Inputs are the resources that go into a program or intervention—what we invest. They include financial, personnel, and in-kind resources from any source. For example, inputs could include time, money, people, equipment, etc. They are materials that the organization or program takes in and then processes to produce the results desired by the organization. Types of inputs are people, money, equipment, facilities, supplies, people's ideas, people's time, etc. Inputs can also be major forces that influence the organization or programs. For example, the inputs to a nonprofit program that provides training to clients might include learners, training materials, teachers, classrooms, funding, paper and pencils, etc. Various laws and regulations effect how the program is conducted, for example, safety regulations, Equal Opportunity Employment guidelines, etc. Inputs are often associated with a cost to obtain and use the item -- budgets are listings of inputs and the costs to obtain and/or use them.

Activities (or Strategies or Methods) are events undertaken by the program or partners to produce desired outcomes—

Intentional Diversity Transformation

what we do. You could include a clear identification of "early" activities and "later" activities. Examples of activities include: conducting workshops, developing products and services, etc.

Activities are used by the organization or program to manipulate and arrange items to produce the results desired by the organization or program or initiative. Processes can range from putting a piece of paper on a desk to manufacturing a space shuttle. However, logic models are usually only concerned with the major recurring processes associated with producing the results desired by the organization or program or initiative. For example, the major processes used by a nonprofit program that provides training to clients might include recruitment of learners, pretesting of learners, training, post-testing and certification.

Intentional Diversity Transformation

Outputs are the direct, tangible results of activities—what we get. These early work products often serve as documentation of progress. They are usually accounted for by their number, for example, the number of students who failed or passed a test, courses taught, tests taken, teachers used, etc. Outputs are frequently misunderstood to indicate success of an organization or program. However, if the outputs aren't directly associated with achieving the benefits desired for stakeholders, then the outputs are poor indicators of the success of the organization and its programs/initiatives. You can use many teachers, but that won't mean that many participants were successfully trained. Examples include: Target group trained, products developed, etc.

Outcomes – this section allows you to describe the ***Short-term***, ***Intermediate***, and ***Long-term*** Outcomes of the initiative. Outcomes are the desired results of the program—what we achieved. Describing outcomes as short, intermediate, or long term depends on the objective, the length of the program, and expectations of the program or intervention. What is identified as a long-term outcome for one program could be an intermediate outcome for another.

Intentional Diversity Transformation

Outcomes		
Short-Term Outcomes	Intermediate Outcomes	Long-Term Outcomes

Short-term Outcomes are the immediate effects of the program or intervention activities. They often focus on the knowledge and attitudes of the intended audience. Examples include: increasing knowledge, increasing competence, increasing skills, improving attitudes, etc. ***Intermediate Outcomes*** are behaviors and/or policy changes. They are the (hopefully positive) impacts on those people whom the organization wanted to benefit with its programs or initiatives. Outcomes are usually specified in terms of: a) learning, including enhancements to knowledge, understanding/perceptions/attitudes, and behaviors

Intentional Diversity Transformation

b) skills (behaviors to accomplish results, or capabilities)
c) conditions (increased security, stability, pride, etc.). They represent the next level in the evolution of a "Short-term Outcome". ***Long-term Outcomes*** refer to the desired results of the program and can take years to accomplish. Long-term outcomes include results such as percentage increase the organization or the group has achieved in ethnic market share. Or, becoming the leader in competitive market share with your industry. They represent the next level in the evolution of an "Intermediate Outcome".

- **Strategic Impact** – this section allows you to describe the ***specific Intended Results*** the Diversity and Inclusion initiative was designed to deliver. It refers to the ultimate impact(s) of the Diversity and Inclusion program or initiative. They could be achieved in a year or take 10 or more years to achieve. Strategic Impact is the fundamental intended or unintended change occurring in organizations, communities or systems as a result of your DEI program activities within 7 to 10 years.

Intentional Diversity Transformation

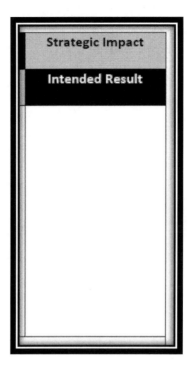

So, How Do You Read the Full Logic Model?

When "read" from left to right, logic models describe program basics over time from planning through results. Reading a logic model means following the chain of reasoning or "If...then..." statements which connect the program or Diversity and Inclusion initiative's parts.

Intentional Diversity Transformation

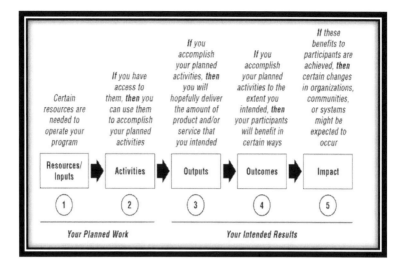

- **Diversity Transformational Analytics** – this section allows you to list the Descriptive, Predictive, and Prescriptive metrics and analytics at each stage of the initiative's workstream along with **"Target Setting"** benchmarks, **"Your Score"**, **"DROI%"**, **"Benefit-to-Cost Ratio"**, and **"Payback Period"**.

Diversity Transformational Analytics								
* Descriptive * Predictive * Prescriptive								
Target Setting			Your Score					
Green	Yellow	Red	Outstanding	Excellent	Good	Fair	Poor
641 - 1000	400 - 640	399 - Below	851 - 1000	641 - 850	500 - 640	400 - 499	399 - Below

Intentional Diversity Transformation

DROI %	BCR	Payback Period

- **Assumptions, External Factors, & Contingencies** – this section allows you to indicate assumptions and external factors as well as contingencies that will affect the Diversity and Inclusion initiative during its implementation.

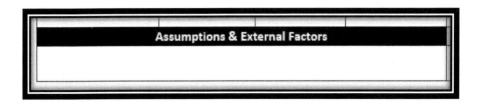

Assumptions & External Factors

Assumptions are the beliefs we have about the program or intervention and the resources involved. Assumptions include the way we think the Diversity and Inclusion program or initiative will work—the "theory" we have used to develop the program or intervention. Assumptions are based on research, best practices, past experience and common sense. The decisions we make about implementing a program or intervention are often based on our assumptions. Examples of assumptions we sometimes make include:

Intentional Diversity Transformation

- Funding will be secure throughout the course of the Diversity and Inclusion project or intervention.
- Because we teach information, it will be adopted and used in the way we intended.
- Employees and others will be motivated to attend learning sessions.
- External funds and well-placed change agents can facilitate institutional change.
- Staff with the necessary skills and abilities can be recruited and hired.
- Partnerships or coalitions can effectively address problems or reach into areas we cannot.
- Policy adoption leads to individual behavior change.

In developing your Hubbard Intentional Diversity Transformation Scorecard® logic model, you should explore and discuss the assumptions you are making. Often, an in-depth discussion is included as a narrative that accompanies your Hubbard Intentional Diversity Transformation Scorecard®. Inaccurate or overlooked assumptions could be a reason that your program or intervention did not achieve the expected level of success.

Contextual and External Factors describe the environment in which the Diversity and Inclusion program or initiative exists and outside factors that interact with and influence the program or intervention. These factors may influence implementation, participation, and the achievement of outcomes. ***Contextual*** and ***External factors*** are the conditions over which we have little or no control that affect success.

Examples include:
- Competing or supporting initiatives sponsored by other agencies.
- Socioeconomic factors of the target audience.
- The motivations and behavior of the target population.
- Social norms and conditions that either support or hinder your outcomes in reaching disparate populations, such as the background and personal experiences of participants.
- Politics that support or hinder your activities.
- Potential barriers or supports that could affect the success of your project.

In Diversity and Inclusion program or intervention planning and development, it is always important to consider contextual factors that are likely to affect your activities and either address them or collect data on them as part of the process evaluating the impact of

Intentional Diversity Transformation

your Hubbard Intentional Diversity Transformation Scorecard® and/or when reporting results to stakeholders.

Hubbard & Hubbard, Inc. offers **_DROI® Certification Workshops and Webinars_** to train Diversity & Inclusion Professionals in a wide-range of topics. Certification Workshops to learn how to Analyze, Design, Develop, Implement and Evaluate a Hubbard Intentional Diversity Transformation Scorecard® are scheduled regularly. Please check our Hubbard & Hubbard, Inc. Master Catalog and Schedule of Workshops and Webinars at https://attendee.gototraining.com/5975q/catalog/8188167925517902080?tz=America/Denver

When should the Hubbard Intentional Diversity Transformation Scorecard® be Used?

The Hubbard Intentional Diversity Transformation Scorecard® is useful for both new and existing programs and initiatives. If your Diversity and Inclusion initiative is being planned, the Hubbard Intentional Diversity Transformation Scorecard® can help get it off to a good start. Alternatively, if the Diversity and Inclusion program or initiative is already under way, a Hubbard Intentional Diversity Transformation Scorecard® approach can help you describe, modify or enhance it.

Intentional Diversity Transformation

Employee Resource Group or Business Resource Group Leaders, planners, program managers, trainers, evaluators, advocates and other stakeholders can use a logic model scorecard in several ways throughout an initiative. One model may serve more than one purpose, or it may be necessary to create different versions tailored for different aims. Here are examples of the various times that a logic model could be used.

During planning to:

- clarify program strategy
- identify appropriate outcome targets (and avoid over-promising)
- align your efforts with those of other organizations
- write a grant proposal or a request for proposals
- assess the potential effectiveness of an approach
- set priorities for allocating resources
- estimate timelines
- identify necessary partnerships
- negotiate roles and responsibilities
- focus discussions and make planning time more efficient

Intentional Diversity Transformation

During implementation to:

- provide an inventory of what you have and what you need to operate the program or initiative
- develop a management plan
- incorporate findings from research and demonstration projects
- make mid-course adjustments
- reduce or avoid unintended effects

During staff and stakeholder orientation to:

- explain how the overall program works
- show how different people can work together
- define what each person is expected to do
- indicate how one would know if the program is working

During evaluation to:

- document accomplishments
- organize evidence about the program
- identify differences between the ideal program and its real operation
- determine which concepts will (and will not) be measured

Intentional Diversity Transformation

- frame questions about attribution (of cause and effect) and contribution (of initiative components to the outcomes)
- specify the nature of questions being asked
- prepare reports and other media
- tell the story of the program or initiative

During advocacy to:

- justify why the program will work
- explain how resource investments will be used

The Table below describes the relationship between a successful Diversity and Inclusion program or initiative, and the benefits derived from the use of a logic model approach.

Program Elements	Criteria for Program Success	Benefits of Program Logic Models
Planning and Design	Diversity and Inclusion program goals and objectives, and	Find "gaps" in the theory or logic of a Diversity and Inclusion program

Intentional Diversity Transformation

Program Elements	Criteria for Program Success	Benefits of Program Logic Models
	important side effects are defined ahead of time	or initiative and work to resolve them.
	Program goals and objectives are both plausible and possible	Builds a shared understanding of what the Diversity and Inclusion program or initiative is about and how the parts work together.
Diversity and Inclusion Program or Initiative Implementation and Management	Relevant, credible, and useful performance data can be obtained.	Focuses attention of the group on the most important connections between action and results.
Evaluation, Communication, and Marketing	The intended users of the Intentional Diversity Transformation Scorecard's results	Provides a way to involve and engage stakeholders in the design, processes, and the use of the

Page 225

Intentional Diversity Transformation

Program Elements	Criteria for Program Success	Benefits of Program Logic Models
	have agreed on how they will use the information. Everyone is working towards accomplishing the Strategic Impact.	Transformation Diversity Scorecard.

What are the benefits and limitations of the Hubbard Intentional Diversity Transformation Scorecard®?

You can probably envision a variety of ways in which you might use the Hubbard Intentional Diversity Transformation Scorecard® you've developed or that this logic modeling approach would benefit your work.

Here are a few advantages that experienced users of logic models have discovered.

- **Logic models integrate planning, implementation, and evaluation.** As a detailed description of your initiative, from resources to results, the logic model is equally

Page
226

important for planning, implementing, and evaluating a Diversity and Inclusion program or initiative. If you are a strategic planner, the modeling process challenges you to think more like an evaluator. If your purpose is evaluation, the modeling prompts discussion of DEI strategic planning. And for those who implement, the modeling process answers practical questions about how the work will be organized and managed.

- **Logic models prevent mismatches between activities and effects.** DEI Strategic Planners often summarize an effort by listing its vision, mission, objectives, strategies and action plans. Even with this information, it can be hard to tell how all the pieces fit together. By connecting activities and effects, a logic model helps avoid proposing activities with no intended effect, or anticipating effects with no supporting activities. The ability to spot such mismatches easily is perhaps the main reason why so many logic models use a flow chart format.

- **Logic models leverage the power of partnerships.** Refining a logic model is an iterative or repeating process that allows leaders, diverse work-teams, ERGs/BRGs, and other participants to "make changes based on consensus-building and a logical process rather than on personalities, politics, or ideology. The clarity of thinking that occurs from the process of building the model becomes an important part of the overall success of the program." With a well-specified logic model such as the Hubbard Intentional Diversity Transformation Scorecard®, it is possible to note where the baton should be passed from one person or team to another. This enhances collaboration and guards against things falling through the cracks.

- **Logic models enhance accountability by keeping stakeholders focused on outcomes.** A list of action steps usually function as a manager's guide for running a project, showing what staff or others need to do. With a logic model, however, it is also possible to illustrate the effects of those tasks. This short-term effect then connects to mid- and longer-term effects.

In a coalition or collaborative partnership, logic models make it clear which effects each partner creates and how all those effects converge to a common goal. The family or nesting approach works well in a collaborative partnership because a model can be developed for each objective along a sequence of effects, thereby showing layers of contributions and points of intersection.

Intentional Diversity Transformation

- **Logic models help planners to set priorities for allocating resources**. A comprehensive model will reveal where physical, financial, human, and other resources are needed. When DEI strategic planners are discussing options and setting priorities, a logic model can help them make resource-related decisions in light of how the program's activities and outcomes will be affected.

- **Logic models reveal data needs and provide a framework for interpreting results.** It is possible to design a documentation system that includes only beginning and end measurements. This is a risky strategy with a good chance of yielding disappointing results. An alternative approach calls for tracking changes at each step along the planned sequence of effects like the approach used in the Hubbard Intentional Diversity Transformation Scorecard®. With a logic model, DEI strategic planners and program planners can identify intermediate effects and define measurable indicators for them.

- **Logic models enhance learning by integrating research findings and practice wisdom**. Most Diversity and Inclusion initiatives are founded on assumptions about the behaviors and conditions that need to change, and how they are subject to intervention. Frequently, there are different degrees of certainty about those assumptions. For example, some of the links in a logic model may have been tested and proved to be sound through previous research. Other linkages, by contrast, may never have been researched, indeed may never have been tried or thought of before. The explicit form of a logic model means that you can combine evidence-based practices from prior research with innovative ideas that veteran Diversity and Inclusion practitioners believe will make a difference. *If you are armed with a logic model, it won't be easy for critics to claim that your work is not evidence-based.*

- **Logic models define a shared language and shared vision for organizational change**. The terms used in a logic model help to standardize the way people think and how they speak about organizational change. It gets everyone rowing in the same direction, and enhances communication with external audiences, such as customers or community groups. Even stakeholders who are skeptical or antagonistic toward your work can be drawn into the discussion and development of a logic model. *Once you've got them talking about the logical connections between activities and effects, they're no longer criticizing from the sidelines.* They'll be engaged in problem-solving and they'll be doing so in an open forum, where everyone can see their resistance to change or lack of logic if that's the case.

Limitations

Any tool this powerful must not be approached lightly. When you undertake the task of developing the Hubbard Intentional Diversity Transformation Scorecard®, be aware of the following challenges and limitations.

First, no matter how logical your model seems, there is always a danger that it will not be correct. The world sometimes works in surprising, counter-intuitive ways, which means we may not comprehend the logic of change until after the fact. With this in mind, Hubbard Intentional Diversity Transformation Scorecard® modelers will appreciate the fact that the **real effects** of intervention actions could differ from the *intended effects*. Certain actions might even make problems worse, so it's important to keep one eye on the plan and another focused on the *real-life experiences* of organizational members.

If nothing else, a logic model ought to be logical. Therein lies its strength and its weakness. Those who are trying to follow your logic will magnify any inconsistency or inaccuracy. This places a high burden on Hubbard Intentional Diversity Transformation

Intentional Diversity Transformation

Scorecard® modelers to pay attention to detail and refine their own thinking to great degree. Of course, no model can be perfect. You'll have to decide on the basis of stakeholders' uses what level of precision is required. Working jointly with an experienced diverse work team to create the Hubbard Intentional Diversity Transformation Scorecard® reduces the chances the logic will be inaccurate.

Establishing the appropriate boundaries of a logic model can be a difficult challenge. In most cases, there is a tension between focusing on a specific program and situating that effort within its broader context. Many models seem to suggest that the only forces of change come from within the program in question, as if there is only one child in the sandbox.

At the other extreme, it would be ridiculous and unproductive to map all the simultaneous forces of change that affect the organization's growth and development. A Hubbard Intentional Diversity Transformation Scorecard® modeler's challenge is to include enough depth so the organizational context is clear, without losing sight of the reasons for developing a logic model approach in the first place.

Intentional Diversity Transformation

On a purely practical level, logic modeling can also be time consuming, requiring much energy in the beginning and continued attention throughout the life of a Diversity and Inclusion initiative. The process can demand a high degree of specificity; it risks oversimplifying complex relationships and relies on the skills of the diverse team(s) constructing the model to convey complex thought processes. This is why Hubbard & Hubbard, Inc. offers training and certification on an ongoing basis in this tool and system's application.

Indeed, Hubbard Intentional Diversity Transformation Scorecard® logic models can be challenging to create, ***but the process of creating them, as well as the resulting product, will yield many benefits over the life of a Diversity and Inclusion initiative.***

In Summary

A Hubbard Intentional Diversity Transformation Scorecard® logic model is a story or picture of how a Diversity and Inclusion effort or initiative is supposed to work. The process of developing the Hubbard Intentional Diversity Transformation Scorecard® model brings together stakeholders to articulate the goals of a Diversity and Inclusion program or initiative and the values that support it. It also identifies strategies and desired outcomes of the initiative.

Intentional Diversity Transformation

The Hubbard Intentional Diversity Transformation Scorecard® logic model serves as a means to communicate a program visually within your coalition or work group and to external audiences. It provides a common language and reference point for everyone involved in the initiative.

A Hubbard Intentional Diversity Transformation Scorecard® logic model is useful for planning, implementing and evaluating an initiative. It helps stakeholders agree on short-term as well as long-term objectives during the planning process, outline activities and contributors, and establish clear criteria for evaluation during the effort. When the Diversity and Inclusion initiative ends, it provides a framework for assessing overall effectiveness of the initiative, as well as the activities, resources, and external factors that played a role in the outcome.

To develop a Hubbard Intentional Diversity Transformation Scorecard® model, you will probably use both forward and reverse logic. Working backwards, you begin with the desired outcomes and then identify the strategies and resources that will accomplish them. Combining this with forward logic, you will choose certain steps to produce the desired effects.

Intentional Diversity Transformation

You will probably revise the Hubbard Intentional Diversity Transformation Scorecard® model periodically, and that is precisely one advantage to using a logic model. Because it relates program activities to their effect, it helps keep stakeholders focused on achieving outcomes, while it remains flexible and open to finding the best means to enact a unique story of change.

References

Hubbard, Edward E. *Measuring Diversity Results.* Petaluma, CA: Global Insights, 1997

Hubbard, Edward E. *How to Calculate Diversity Return on Investment.* Petaluma, CA: Global Insights, 1999.

Hubbard, Edward E. *The Diversity Scorecard.* Petaluma, CA: Elsevier Butterworth-Heinemann, 2004.

Hubbard, Edward E. *The Manager's Pocket Guide to Diversity Management.* Amherst, MA: HRD Press, 2003

Kaplan, Robert S.; Norton, David P.. The Strategy-Focused Organization: How Balanced Scorecard Companies Thrive in the New Business Environment (Kindle Locations 1177-1181). Harvard Business Review Press. Kindle Edition.

Kaplan, Robert S.; Norton, David P.. Strategy Maps: Converting Intangible Assets into Tangible Outcomes (Kindle Locations 99-114). Harvard Business Review Press. Kindle Edition.

Kaplan, Robert S.; Norton, David P.. The Strategy-Focused Organization: How Balanced Scorecard Companies Thrive in the New Business Environment (Kindle Locations 1248-1253). Harvard Business Review Press. Kindle Edition.

Kaplan, Robert S.; Norton, David P.. The Strategy-Focused Organization: How Balanced Scorecard Companies Thrive in the New Business Environment (Kindle Locations 1266-1271). Harvard Business Review Press. Kindle Edition.

Kaplan, Robert S.; Norton, David P.. Strategy Maps: Converting Intangible Assets into Tangible Outcomes (Kindle Locations 3213-3220). Harvard Business Review Press. Kindle Edition.

Kaplan, Robert S.; Norton, David P.. Strategy Maps: Converting Intangible Assets into Tangible Outcomes (Kindle Locations 3220-3227). Harvard Business Review Press. Kindle Edition.

Chapter Seven: Strategies to Implement and Track Transformational Diversity Scorecard Initiatives

Strategies for Implementing Your Hubbard Intentional Diversity Transformation Scorecard®

Developing a Hubbard Intentional Diversity Transformation Scorecard® and actually implementing one are two different things. It requires a planned, strategic approach that involves all levels within the organization. This chapter explains how to build a systemic process to drive your Transformation Diversity Scorecard, that is, how to be disciplined in applying lessons of transformational change management to the implementation of the Diversity

Intentional Diversity Transformation

Scorecard you develop. It serves less as a road map to what is on the Scorecard and more as a guide to implementing the Scorecard and generating transformational results. It links and aligns with the processes that drive the evidence-based outcomes of your Diversity initiatives for a measurable strategic impact.

Group Name:	
Initiative Name:	
Goal(s)/Objectives	
Strategies &Tactics	
Measures &Targets **With Stoplight Levels**	

Intentional Diversity Transformation

Action Plans	
Systems/Process Integration Actions	
Expected Outcomes	
Benefits/Value-Added	
Comments/Notes	

Intentional Diversity Transformation

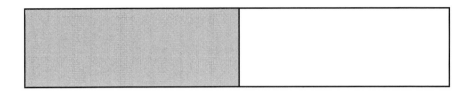

Initiative Identification – this section allows you to identify the specific Diversity, Equity and Inclusion (DEI) department or Employee Resource or Business Resource Group (ERG/BRG) implementing the strategic Diversity or Inclusion initiative. It also highlights the Initiative's name as well as its targeted goals and objectives.

Intentional Diversity Transformation

Group Name:	
Initiative Name:	
Goal(s)/Objectives	

Strategic Initiative Plan Alignment Components – this section allows you to align the DEI Department or ERG/BRG implementation plan actions and components such as:

- Strategies & Tactics
- Measures & Targets with Stoplight Levels
- Action Plans
- Systems/Process Integration Actions

Intentional Diversity Transformation

Strategies & Tactics	
Measures & Targets With Stoplight Levels	
Action Plans	
Systems/Process Integration Actions	

Strategic Outcomes and Impact Planning Components – this section allows you to focus on and construct:

- Expected outcomes that match C-suite and other stakeholder needs and,
- "Value-added" financial/non-financial benefits which make a measurable difference in the organization's performance.
- Comments/Notes that chronicle key ideas related to this action plan you do not want to forget.

Intentional Diversity Transformation

Expected Outcomes	
Benefits/Value-Added	
Comments/Notes	

Planning and structuring your initiatives in this way creates a "line-of-sight" to the targeted outcome you desire. This approach will help transform the organization's functioning in a way that delivers intentional evidence-based results and impact that is credible and sustainable. My life's work has been to create the "***Sciences***" side of the Diversity and Inclusion discipline (every discipline, whether its Marketing, Sales, Operations, etc. has both "theory" and "science"). Many years ago, when I started working in DEI, there were no sciences, only theory. My goal was to provide Diversity,

Equity and Inclusion Practitioners with next level, research and evidence-based methods that are measurable, credible, reliable and sustainable! The approaches in this book are an element of the Hubbard Diversity and Inclusion Sciences and its associated DEI ROI-based Methodologies and disciplines, advanced Metrics and Analytics, frameworks, tools, templates, worksheets, automated online ROI-based Dashboards, Scorecards, Calculators, apps, assessments, and much more.

References

Basarab, D. J., Predictive Evaluation: Ensuring Training Delivers Business and Organizational Results. San Francisco, CA: Berrett-Koehler Publishers, 2011.

Hubbard, Edward E. *Diversity Return on Investment (DROI®) Fundamentals: Ensuring Diversity Initiatives Demonstrate ROI Impact Value on the Bottom-line.* Petaluma, CA: Global Insights Publishing, 2014.

Hubbard, Edward E. *How to Calculate Diversity Return on Investment.* Petaluma, CA: Global Insights, 1999.

Hubbard, Edward E. *Measuring Diversity Results.* Petaluma, CA: Global Insights, 1997.

Hubbard, Edward E., Hubbard, *Measuring the ROI Impact of ERGs and BRGs: Ensuring Employee Resource Group Initiatives Drive Business and Organizational Results*. Petaluma, CA: Global Insights, 2014.

Chapter Eight: Predictive Analytics for Diversity (PAD$_{tm}$) - A Next Practice Approach

Introduction

The Predictive Analytics for Diversity^{tm} (PAD) Framework, as a critical component of the Intentional Diversity Scorecard®, offers guidance for succeeding on a day-to-day basis. It equips Diversity Professionals and Diversity Practitioners with an essential resource, and mental model to drive Diversity Return on Investment performance outcomes and impacts. Whether you're a Chief Diversity Officer, Diversity Director, Diversity and Inclusion Trainer, Diversity Analyst, member of a Diversity Council, member of an Employee Resource Group/Business Resource Group, or a part of a seasoned or newly created Diversity staff function, this chapter presents a pragmatic, how-to guide which gives you the answers to

Intentional Diversity Transformation

define and drive best practices in Diversity metrics and ROI analytics.

Predictive Analytics for Diversity^{tm} (PAD) is a new approach that provides compelling Diversity investment return data to executives, including (1) predicting success of Diversity initiatives and interventions in the three areas of Intention, Adoption, and Impact which allow you to measure to see if success has been achieved; (2) leading indicators of future adoption (transfer of learning and behaviors) and Impact (achieving sustainable business results); and (3) making recommendations for continuous performance improvement. PAD has two major components:

- *Predicting,* which is before-the-fact, to decide whether to implement the Diversity initiative, and
- *Evaluating,* which is an after-the-fact measurement against the predictions.

The beauty of PAD is that it uses leading measures (Intention and Adoption) as a signal of results (Impact). If the leading indicators are below predicted success thresholds, actions can be implemented to make critical adjustments so that the desired results are realized. (adapted from Basarab, 2011)

Intentional Diversity Transformation

Benefits of Predictive Analytics for Diversity[tm]

What are the benefits of PAD? You now can predict (forecast) Diversity and Inclusion's value to the organization, measure against those predictions, use leading indicators to ensure that you are on track, and report in a business format that executives easily understand. You can interweave outcomes and leading indicators into Diversity and Inclusion interventions during the design and implementation phases and move from an event-driven function to one that predicts success, measures its performance against those predictions, and is seen as returning significant shareholder value for the funds invested.

However, the greatest strength of the Predictive Analytics for Diversity[tm] (PAD) approach is not about how it is communicated to the executives, or the tools, or the results, but rather how it requires participation of the supervisors and the employees in setting their *own* intentions and measurement of adoption. The approach treats the employees as adults owning their role and part in the Diversity intervention versus as passive participants checking off the boxes from their list and being measured by someone else.

The key components of the approach are the ***Diversity and Inclusion initiatives***, ***the Diversity and Inclusion outcomes***,

Intentional Diversity Transformation

prediction of value, ***Intention*** (to use), ***Adoption*** (actual use), and ***Impact*** the results delivered to the organization).

Where to Start

The Predictive Analytics for Diversity[tm] (PAD) starts with an existing Diversity or Inclusion initiative or one that is on the drawing board. In other words, the Predictive Analytics for Diversity[tm] (PAD) approach works for both existing initiatives or interventions and new ones in the production queue. PAD is independent of an initiative's delivery-it works equally well for classroom-based training, on-the-job action plans and intervention implementation, culture change initiatives, innovation interventions, online learning, simulations, workshops, etc. The approach works with different content. PAD has been conducted on Leadership initiatives, Sales Training and initiatives, Business Management programs, and Basic Management interventions. PAD is also independent of audience and has been used for groups from senior executives to hourly employees. Finally, PAD can be employed for programs and interventions that are developed and delivered in-house (those where the company has internal personnel create and deliver the intervention) or outsourced programs (those

Intentional Diversity Transformation

purchased from external vendors to meet a company's business performance goals and objectives).

To begin a PAD process on an existing program or initiative, you need to obtain and review the intervention design documents, program and/or initiative materials, any existing evaluation data (such as Evaluation Level 1 survey results), budget (actual expenses and projected expenses), number and types of employees already trained, the number of employees who need training in the future, targeted outcomes, etc. This is only the starting point-you can gather other information, such as opinions from initiative participants, their supervisors, suppliers, and executives who sponsor the program or initiative. The purpose is to thoroughly understand and describe the object being evaluated (the Diversity and Inclusion intervention and/or initiative). Once you understand the intervention, you can begin the predictive portion of PAD.

But the best place to start a PAD effort is on an initiative that is still on the drawing board. You don't start PAD with the initiative design process, it comes in as a component to ensure that the Diversity and Inclusion initiative design creates the proper transformational value and impact the company needs. In many initiative design processes, *Evaluate* is the final stage of the process. PAD starts before the

Intentional Diversity Transformation

program or initiative finalizes its design, using its predictive components, and is an input/requirement for the final intervention design.

Typically, the predictive portion of PAD begins for new initiatives when the **Analysis** and **Design** phases of the intervention are completed. In the **Analysis** phase, the intervention or initiative problem is clarified, the intervention goals and objectives are established, and the learning/performance environment and participant's existing knowledge and skills are identified. The **Design** phase deals with the initiative objectives, assessment instruments, exercises, content, subject matter analysis, action planning, implementation strategies, and media selection.

Whether the Diversity and Inclusion initiative to be evaluated currently exists or is still under design, the PAD approach makes the assumption that all interventions and programs are designed to provide participants and the organization with the following benefits:

- **Knowledge**: either new knowledge or a refresher of current knowledge
- **Skills**: new or improved techniques for getting work done

Intentional Diversity Transformation

- **Beliefs**: the idea that the participants and/or the organization can benefit from using the new knowledge and skills
- **Behaviors**: On-the-job practices and habits that shift or are adopted to improve actions and thinking that impact business

The Predictive Analytics for Diversity^{tm} Framework

Let's take a minute to examine the methodology and premise which supports the Predictive Analytics for Diversity^{tm} (PAD) Framework to better understand how it works. Before, during, and after participants leave a Diversity initiative or intervention, they have some level of motivation to use what they learned. These levels of motivation are called "**intentions**". Intentions can vary in strength from "very weak" to "very strong". On the basis of their intentions, participants in the Diversity initiative or intervention "**adopt**" (apply) the new skills and behaviors as part of their normal work routine or process. Adopted behaviors practiced over time (repetition) produce results (an "**impact**") for the organization. The magnitude and value of the results are affected by all three factors: (1) Intention, (2) Adoption, and (3) Impact. Using this as a basis for reflecting an employee's learning and performance, we can predict

Intention, Adoption, and ultimately Impact. However, before we are able to do that we need to understand the three factors that make up this framework in more detail.

Intention Evaluation

An Intention Evaluation (IE) addresses the following question: *"At the end of the Diversity initiative or intervention, are the goals and beliefs of the diverse participants who are involved in the Diversity initiative or intervention aligned with the desired goals"*? **Intentions** are the goals that participants wish to achieve using the knowledge and skills they learned during the initiative and supported by their beliefs. This is the first focus point, because there is little or no adoption or business impact if participants have little or no intent to use the knowledge, skills, or behaviors learned during the Diversity initiative or intervention. Intention Evaluation involves judging participant authored-goals against a predefined standard. If participant goals meet the standard, those goals are labeled as acceptable. Goals that do not meet the standard are labeled as unacceptable.

At this point, an "Intention Success Gate", which is the percentage of acceptable goals, is predicted (e.g., 90 percent). Intention data is collected from participants via a goal planning worksheet during the

Intentional Diversity Transformation

initiative or intervention and submitted, after the initiative to the Diversity Performance Consultant/Evaluator, who judges each goal as acceptable or unacceptable (Hubbard & Hubbard, Inc. conducts Diversity Performance Consultant/Evaluator Certification Programs throughout the year in public sessions and in virtual "1:1 formats". Paste the following link in a browser: https://attendee.gototraining.com/5975q/catalog/8188167925517902080?tz=America/Denver) to learn when Certification workshops are held. This in turn creates an **"Intention Score"** (percentage of goals judged acceptable). When the Intention Score exceeds the Success Gate, the intervention or initiative is deemed successful (in creating the proper Intentions). If the Intentions Score is below the gate, an analysis of why and what can be done to improve the results is undertaken. *Intention data are leading indicators to **Adoption*** (transferring knowledge and skills from the Diversity Initiative or Intervention to the job). When Intention Scores meet Success Gate standards, there is a higher likelihood that the goals will be adopted. The following are some questions and things to consider about Intention goals.

- *Are these goals supposed to be based on the goals that are developed by the stakeholders or initiative owners?* **Answer:** Yes.

Intentional Diversity Transformation

- *Do the participants get to use those as the basis for developing their own goals?* **Answer:** It is a good idea to share sample goals with participants so that they see how to construct a good goal. It also may stir their thinking on what they want to do.

- *Why do they author their own? Why don't they just use the ones designed by the stakeholders and write the "how" of implementation in their area?* **Answer:** by authoring their goal in their own words, they are creating their personal action plan. It leverages the value of Inclusion of the participant's knowledge and experience as well strengthens their belief and motivation to complete the goal. This is also a method of determining how committed they are to implement the skills necessary to drive Adoption, which leads to predicted Impact. If participants are given the list of stakeholder goals, you are simply testing the ability to choose versus understanding do they have what it takes and the commitment to perform the work.

- *Can Diversity Evaluators or Initiative Instructors help them with their goals?* **Answer:** absolutely. A best practice is having the participant draft the goal(s), have it reviewed by the *Diversity Evaluator or Initiative*

Intentional Diversity Transformation

Instructor, then finalize it. Some initiatives and interventions support the practice of participants sharing their goals with each other—giving and receiving feedback to make the goals better.

- *What if the goals they come up with are completely different than the designer's intentions?* **Answer:** some analysis needs to be conducted to determine why this has happened. Typical causes are (1) the intervention or initiative taught or reinforced the wrong things, (2) the initiative or intervention was not designed well enough to teach what is needed, (3) the participants are not from the target group or population that needs to learn or obtain this knowledge or need to learn these behaviors and skills, therefore they would have difficulty writing a good goal, (4) the participants are weak goal writers. Once the causes are identified, corrective actions can be implemented to eliminate or greatly reduce these issues.

The following are a few examples of well-written Intention Goals:

- To build a more open, collaborative team environment, I will show a more positive attitude, because I tend to be a grump the first couple of hours in the morning. I will smile and thank my team for their

Intentional Diversity Transformation

input. I will also ask open-ended questions to gain their point of view during our daily morning meetings. The outcome I expect is that my team members will feel they are valued and will become more motivated/happy to do their work and feel that they have a sense of accomplishment.

- I will be more patient in everyday tasks and when working with my coworkers and other departments by being open to new ideas, asking open-ended questions, listening, and using a positive attitude. The outcome I expect is to have a fun work environment and to show people that it is great to speak up about concerns.

- Make sure that at least once a week I give the ERG/BRG member groups and/or Diversity & Inclusion Department teams a chance to hold an executive briefing. I will mentor them on how to hold a top notch briefing on strategic business objectives aligned with business goals and give them feedback regarding what specifically works well and things to avoid. The outcome I expect is for them to become more involved and give input and build their confidence, resulting in improved performance in key business initiative areas.

Belief Evaluation

Beliefs are defined as "the idea that the participant and/or their organization will benefit from using the new knowledge and skills." Belief data are also captured during goal creation but do not need to be associated with a specific goal. Beliefs are derived from the initiative or intervention design and/or content and are answers to the question – *"What do our employees need to believe so that they successfully transfer the Diversity initiative knowledge, skills and behaviors to the job"*? The following are a few brief examples:

- When leading people, my attitude makes a difference.
- I have a voice and can make a difference in the outcome and impact.
- I own the customer experience.
- Values drive results.
- A fun workplace drives productivity.

Participant belief data are captured on the goal planning worksheet by having participants rate how meaningful the beliefs are to them. Typically a 7-point sematic differential scale is used, where 1=Meaningless and 7=Meaningful. As with goals, a Success Gate for beliefs is predicted, for example, 90 percent of the participants will rate beliefs as *"top box"* (*a 6 or 7 on the 7-point scale*). If the Success Gate is achieved, the Diversity or Inclusion initiative is successful from a Belief Evaluation standpoint. If results are below the gate, the Diversity or Inclusion initiative is viewed as unsuccessful and an investigation and/or corrective actions are implemented.

When the Intention Scores for both *goals and beliefs* meet their respective Success Gates the entire Diversity or Inclusion initiative (for that delivery) is seen as meeting Intention predictions: it is classified as successful. When *either* one of the two Success Gates (Intention or Beliefs) fails to be met, the Diversity or Inclusion Initiative (for that delivery) is seen as unsuccessful.

Corrective actions on Intentions results include redesigning the Diversity or Inclusion initiative, initiative Instructor improvement, making sure participants are from the target population, etc. For the participants who just completed the Diversity or Inclusion initiative and whose goals are below standard, you can work with them one-on-one or in small groups to author the right goals. You can even suggest their supervisors meet with them to beef up the goals so that they are pointed in the right direction for performance and Adoption.

Adoption Evaluation

An **Adoption Evaluation** addresses the following question: "*How much of the Diversity and Inclusion Initiative has been implemented on the job and successfully integrated into the participant's work behavior*"? An Adoption Evaluation analyzes participant performance (that is…behaviors and actions that the employee has transferred to the job) and participant goal completion rate against a defined Adoption Success Gate (percentage of employees performing as predicted). A set of On-the-job adoptive behaviors is developed from the Diversity or Inclusion initiative material or from the Intention goal and belief statements. A few examples of Adoption behaviors include the following:

- Model a positive attitude by relating to coworkers as to what is currently going on with work challenges and reward their positive attitude in solving them.
- Provide positive feedback when contacting my employees and providing recognition on their performance milestones in a manner consistent with their diverse needs and preferences.
- Obtain and enhance Voice of the Customer (VOC) intelligence for existing and potential diverse customers.

Intentional Diversity Transformation

- Estimate revenue, return on investment, and non-financial impact from Diversity and Inclusion initiatives on a quarterly basis, along with annual reports covering these outcome results.

In this case, *you want to know if the Intention goals have been implemented and are sustainable in the workplace*. At this stage, you are evaluating employees who are reporting goal completion – that is…those who have completed their goal or have made significant progress towards completion and whose on-the-job performance is similar to the defined adoptive behaviors. An **Adoption Evaluation** is usually conducted two to three months after participants have completed the Diversity and/or Inclusion initiative, giving them time to attempt, adjust, and finally adopt their new skills, knowledge, and behavior. Adoption data are collected by surveying participants seeking specific transfer to-the-job evidence that is measurable. Environmental factors that have enabled and inhibited Adoption are also collected along with the results (Impact) from the participant's new performance level(s).

An "*Adoption Rate Success Gate*" is set (predicted) defining the percentage of participants who will successfully implement goals that are similar to the adoptive behaviors (performance on the job).

Intentional Diversity Transformation

An example of an Adoption Rate Success Gate is: *60 percent of employees will have successfully implemented one or more of the Diversity or Inclusion initiative adoptive behaviors.* This is the target that the organization expects from the initiative participants based upon stakeholder expectations articulated in the initial initiative Needs Analysis interviews and data collection. If the Success Gate is met, in terms of Adoption Evaluation, the Diversity or Inclusion initiative is deemed successful. If however, the Adoption Rate is below the Success Gate, root cause analysis is conducted, and corrective actions are put in place. These corrections can be for the group that has just been evaluated, to lift its adoption rate, and/or future participants, to ensure that they adopt the right things at the right rate. Examples of corrective actions based upon Adoption Evaluation include the following:

- Review the inhibiting factors and attempt to minimize them. For example, if a large portion of the inhibitors resulted from lack of management support, you could (1) create a "Job-Aid" for managers, with tips for coaching and supporting their employees; (2) change the Initiative attendance policy to require that managers attend the initiative training with their employees to jointly build support plans during the session; (3) require managers to meet with their employees one week after completing the initiative workshop and build the use of the new skills into the employee's annual performance and individual development plan (IDP).

- Maybe an inhibitor is pointing towards insufficient knowledge or skills to do the job correctly. In this case, you could (1) change the initiative design and delivery to enhance the learning of that knowledge and skill; (2) build more in-depth skill practice; (3) pair low performing participants with high-performing participants to job shadow and learn correct application approaches; (4) provide remedial training via job aids, podcasts, micro-learning aids, webinars or gamification tools and strategies; (5) have high performing employees share their success stories with others – what they did, when they did it, and how they did it.

You can also use high-performing participants' success stories as examples of how the initiative strategies can be deployed back on-the-job. These can be shared in workshops and interventions conducted by initiative managers, instructors, or even better, bring the participants to share their stories personally. At times, you can have successful participants mentor new participants.

Intentional Diversity Transformation

Impact Evaluation

An **Impact Evaluation** addresses the following questions: "*What business results can be traced back to the goal adoption of participants*"? "*Are results to the business as predicted*"? "*What is the typical profile of a participant who has achieved results*"? "*What additional business results (value) could be achieved if participants who have little or no adoption were to adopt their goals*"? An Impact Evaluation assesses the changes to organizational results attributable to the use of skills mastered during the initiative training and/or development.

Using the behaviors from the Adoption predictions, you determine the value from one person successfully performing the unit of work. Then, based on the initiative design and business performance requirements (when the participant could and should do the work), you determine how frequently one person should perform the unit of work, based on target audience and work practices (e.g., strategic planning usually has a frequency of once per year; or, using a specific response protocol while working with diverse customers on the phone; would offer numerous opportunities to utilize the new skills. By estimating the number of employees to be trained in the initiative over its life span, noting the Adoption Rate of participants actually performing the correct work, and taking into account that internal and external factors working on the organization contribute to the results, you can predict the Impact that the organization should receive.

Participants identified in the Adoption Evaluation phase, as those who have self-reported as achieving their goals, are surveyed to capture further results and are then interviewed for specific, measurable evidence. Using this Impact data, profiles of participants whose use of the skills have produced the greatest impact are developed. This data, along with an examination of organizational records to show actual value realized, is compiled to build a complete picture of the impact. This becomes the value realized for Impact Evaluation, and when actual results exceed the gate, the Diversity and Inclusion Initiative is successful in delivering on its promised value. If values are below the gate, determining why results are below expectations leads to the necessary corrections (to the initiative, organizational support, etc.).

Predicting the Value of Diversity and Inclusion Initiatives

Now that you have a basic understanding of Intention; Adoption; and Impact Evaluation, let's put it all together by outlining the

Intentional Diversity Transformation

process to predict the value of a Diversity and Inclusion Initiative or Intervention. Predicting the value of a Diversity and Inclusion Initiative or Intervention is similar to the method which business executives use for deciding which piece of equipment to purchase, what products to launch, whether or not to expand the workforce, etc. Lacking sufficient information about the contributions of Diversity & Inclusion initiatives, decision makers could fail to support those Diversity and Inclusion initiatives that have the greatest potential for producing significant value for the organization. When decision makers decide to spend large sums of money on Diversity and Inclusion initiatives, they seek to evaluate their options as they world evaluate other large investments – on basis of financial returns to the organization. The Hubbard Predictive Analytics for Diversity (PAD[tm]) approach allows you to predict results prior to the Diversity and Inclusion initiative delivery (early in the design process), decide whether the benefits (value gained) are worth the investment, and if the choice is to go ahead with the initiative, then evaluate and report its Intention, Beliefs, Adoption, and Impact such that corrective actions are implemented as needed.

Predictive Analytics for Diversity (PAD[tm]) allows you to predict what Impact (results) will be realized by your organization, what

Intentional Diversity Transformation

behaviors will result in Adoptions (transfer) for participants and at what success rate, and what Intentions (goals and beliefs) participants must create, thereby enabling them to begin Adoption.

Working with a team of subject matter experts, staff from various lines of business, Human Resource personnel, Finance personnel, Diversity and Inclusion personnel, target audience members, Diversity Performance Consultants/Technologists, you will create an **"Impact Matrix"** – that is…the prediction of the Diversity and Inclusion initiative's value. The **Impact Matrix** documents the following for the Diversity & Inclusion initiative:

- **Goals** that participants should create during the initiative and the Success Gate
- **Beliefs** that participants should have upon completing the initiative and the Success Gate
- **Adoptive** behaviors and the Success Gate (Adoption Rate)
- **Frequency of adoption**: how often the work is performed
- **Results** of performing the Adoptive behavior
- **External contribution factor**: the percentage that other influences beyond the Diversity & Inclusion initiative contribute to the results

Intentional Diversity Transformation

- The **predicted Impact** that a set of participants will produce over time

Costs to design, develop, maintain, and evaluate the Diversity and Inclusion initiative is calculated for the initiative's life span. This along with the **Impact Matrix** and *initiative design document* are presented to key decision makers to aid in determining whether or not to move forward with the Diversity and Inclusion initiative's investment. The **Hubbard Predictive Analytics for Diversity** (PAD^{tm}) predictions method provides key decision makers with the following:

- A clear picture of the business outcomes
- Outcomes that can be classified and placed in order of importance with other non-Diversity and Inclusion initiative decisions.
- Alternatives that may be explored (e.g., different initiative designs, scope of implementation, non-Diversity and Inclusion solutions to the problem, etc.)

Organizations typically follow a minimum rate of return or payback policy that provides guidance on whether the organization should move forward with any large investment. This is usually provided

Intentional Diversity Transformation

by the Finance department, and the predicted Impact and budget are critical for making informed choice investment decisions.

Diversity and Inclusion's Value and Worth

Adoption and Impact evaluation demonstrate the worth of the Diversity and Inclusion initiative to business executives – by showing the progression of employees from initiative participants to high-performing employees, to generating bottom line results that contribute to the organization's profitable growth.

Merit	Worth	Worth
•*Intention* •Are participant goals and beliefs aligned with desired standards?	•*Adoption* •How much of the Diversity and Inclusion initiative has been implemented and successfully integrated into improved performance on the job?	•*Impact* •Is the Diversity and Inclusion initiative contributing to improved organization results?

This element of the Predictive Analytics for Diversity (PAD^{tm}) approach provides information in a continuous improvement cycle. Data from the first round of Adoption and Impact evaluation are

Intentional Diversity Transformation

used to enhance the likelihood of greater Adoption and greater Impact on future initiatives.

The Predictive Analytics for Diversity (PAD[tm]) process provides data on the merit and worth of Diversity and Inclusion. **Merit** answers the question: *"Does the Diversity and Inclusion initiative do what it is supposed to do"*? **Worth** answers the question: *"Does the initiative add value beyond itself"*? Intention data, goals, and beliefs indicate whether the initiative is working during the initiative or intervention process. In other words, does the initiative (learning experience) create the right intentions in participants? This is considered the merit of the initiative. Adoption and Impact data are considered the worth of the initiative because they show the value of the intervention after the initiative has concluded.

As a result, predicting the Diversity and Inclusion initiative's value helps you understand the meaning and significance of crucial financial impacts that your initiative provides to the organization. It allows key decision makers to use financial analysis to maintain fiscal discipline and to make sound business decisions. It provides a roadmap, via the initiative, to revenue and profit potential. And, it allows you to manage the initiative's overall performance and document its contribution to the organization.

Intentional Diversity Transformation

Why Predictive?

The Predictive Analytics for Diversity (PAD^{tm}) process employs a business model that executives are used to. It provides metrics and analytics that executives and sponsors care about. It forces you to think through the outcomes beyond the Diversity and Inclusion initiative objectives. In fact, predicting results ensure the initiative is aligned with creating business value. The predictions can aid in deciding whether the Diversity and Inclusion investment should be funded. If the benefits (Impact) predicted are not attractive to the organization decision makers, the effort should be stopped.

However, with a solid prediction of the value delivered, decision makers will approve your Diversity and Inclusion effort. Clearly, the Predictive Analytics for Diversity (PAD^{tm}) approach should be included very early in the Diversity and Inclusion initiative development process. It reflects what everyone else in business has to do and if the Diversity and Inclusion organization wants to be credible, it must meet the same standard that other departments are held to.

Intentional Diversity Transformation

The Predictive Analytics for Diversity (PAD™) Sequence

After reviewing this chapter, you should have a basic understanding of the Predictive Analytics for Diversity (PAD™) approach. Below, you will find some typical steps which must be completed to launch the Predictive Analytics for Diversity (PAD™) process.

1. Choose the Diversity and Inclusion initiative you wish to evaluate; it can be a new initiative or an initiative that already exists.

2. Review the initiative to fully understand what it is, what it is supposed to produce, how participants learn and incorporate the knowledge, skills, and behaviors, what business issues it addresses, who is to attend, how they attend, what pre-initiative preparations are required, what post initiative support tools exist, who are the sponsors, what sponsors see as the purpose for the initiative and the sponsors expectations.

3. Form a committee to predict the initiative's value: create the Impact Matrix and present the predictions to key decision makers.

4. Evaluate Intentions: during the initiative pilot and every session thereafter. *Intention Evaluation* improve

Intentional Diversity Transformation

results as necessary by conducting root cause analysis and implementing corrective action.

5. Evaluate Adoption: determine how often and when to conduct *Adoption Evaluation*. Improve results as necessary by conducting root cause analysis and implementing corrective action.

6. Evaluate Impact: determine how often and when to conduct *Impact Evaluations*. Improve results as necessary by conducting root cause analysis and implementing corrective action.

The Predictive Analytics for Diversity (PAD^{tm}) process offers a solid methodology to predict and evaluate the value of Diversity and Inclusion initiatives on the bottom-line. It outlines an extremely credible, science-based methodology that is measurable and evidence-based. It utilizes combined methods from technologies such as the Hubbard Diversity Return on Investment Methodology (DROI®), Predictive Evaluation Sciences, Data Analytics, Lean Six Sigma, etc. The framework is adapted from the seminal evaluation research created by Dave Basarab. His approach to evaluating Training and Development creates a foundational structure which can be applied to many other disciplines.

Intentional Diversity Transformation

The Predictive Analytics for Diversity (PAD^{tm}) process represents a next-level approach to the field of Diversity and Inclusion sciences. It provides a means for Diversity and Inclusion professionals to answer critical outcome based questions such as the following:

- What level of proficiency must Diversity Executives achieve to be seen as a fully capable and credible Business Partner?
- How do I gauge the progress of our organization's Diversity change initiative in business-aligned measurement terms?
- How do I calculate the Diversity Return on Investment (DROI®) impact of our Diversity and Inclusion initiatives that reflect credibility?
- How do I influence decision making for organizational improvement and business results using effective Diversity and Analytic strategies?
- How do I calculate the bottom-line impact and contribution of our initiatives or interventions in business-related terms, and much more.

Using science-based approaches to demonstrate Diversity and Inclusion's impact on business performance allows Diversity and Inclusion to be taken seriously as a critical business partner for organizational success. Our future as a respected profession and discipline depends on it!

References

Basarab, D. J., *Predictive Evaluation: Ensuring Training Delivers Business and Organizational Results.* San Francisco, CA: Berrett-Koehler Publishers, 2011.

Basarab, D. J., & Root, D. The Training Evaluation Process. Boston/Dordrecht/ London: Kluer Academic Publishers. 1992.

Hubbard, Edward E. *Diversity Return on Investment (DROI®) Fundamentals: Ensuring Diversity Initiatives Demonstrate ROI Impact Value on the Bottom-line.* Petaluma, CA: Global Insights Publishing, 2014.

Chapter Nine: Driving the Future of Diversity and Inclusion

As I mentioned in the first chapter of this book, Performance Measurement in organizations is not something new, however in the last 30 years or so, organizations have realized that financial measures alone are not sufficient for evaluating the success of an enterprise. This is especially true when attempts are made to measure and evaluate the impact of Diversity and Inclusion initiatives. We seem to be stuck on measuring Diversity representation as reflective of progress in Diversity. I feel this is a grossly limited view of true Diversity and Inclusion progress.

From a Diversity and Inclusion ROI impact standpoint, D&I progress must be based upon not only "representation" but more specifically on the "*utilization*" of the differences and similarities in people that make a measurable difference in an organization's performance. Representation alone does not create organizational change and transformation, **"utilization"** of our human capital

Intentional Diversity Transformation

assets does (especially in an organization that mandates Inclusion and respect as the context for workforce engagement). The Hubbard Intentional Diversity Transformation Scorecard® and its associated sciences makes possible an integrated, "systems-approach" to create transformative change and value for organizations. It is rooted in validated research and sciences that drive evidence-based outcomes that are accurate and credible. The requirements for Diversity and Inclusion success, now and in the future, will depend on mastering these Diversity and Inclusion ROI Sciences®. Doing so brings standards, rigor, process as well as predictable evidence-based ROI–focused outcomes to the work we do.

I hope you will join our community of dedicated DEI Professionals who strive to create, maintain, and enhance the credibility of our profession with evidence and research-based sciences using the Hubbard Diversity and Inclusion ROI Methodology, Sciences, and Disciplines. We expect other disciplines like Marketing, Sales, Finance, Operations, Engineering and the like to be rooted in proven sciences that we can count on. Diversity, Equity and Inclusion should be NO different! If not, DEI leaves itself open to failed initiatives and interventions that are NOT worth the organization's investment dollars. Unfortunately, I have witnessed organizations investing millions of dollars in DEI initiatives that affect thousands of employees, which are doomed from the start, which fail, and generate more damage to the diverse workforce, the organization, DEI's reputation and its future success. There is a saying by Stephen Covey that states there are three constants in life…**Choice**, **Change**, and **Principles**. The question is will you make the **Choice** to help lift the standards of our discipline by **Changing** to DEI ROI Analytical Science **Principles** and Methods? If so, Hubbard & Hubbard, Inc. Diversity & Inclusion ROI Sciences® can help you earn Certification(s) in these processes.

Futurist Joel A. Barker once stated that "Vision without action is merely a dream. Action without vision just passes the time. Vision with action can change the world." This quote inspires me to examine my intentions behind my actions. Especially in my efforts to create and apply Diversity and Inclusion ROI sciences. Often we can get very busy and yet accomplish nothing. I have found that it is important to "**align my attentions to my intention**". That is, I found that when driving change and transformation in Diversity and Inclusion, it is critical to have passion, commitment and a vision to know where you are going, then take consistent action to move toward your vision. This is what changes our world and creates success. Author and Motivational Speaker Tony Robbins once said:

Intentional Diversity Transformation

"If you talk about it, it's a dream, if you envision it it's possible, but if you schedule it, it's real!"

Using this next-level transformational scorecard approach can significantly advance the impact of Diversity and Inclusion's value for years to come if you schedule its use and implement it. There are no short cuts or skipping steps. Our success in Diversity and Inclusion is predicated upon utilizing all of the proven, scientific tools available to make a measurable difference in the organization's performance. Much of what happens in D&I's success for the future depends on what you do next. Yes, it's hard work and takes discipline to follow the scientific processes involved. However, it's the only credible way to prove and sustain our value as professionals and who can create a measurable investment that is well worth the return!

Other Resources

Diversity ROI Certification Institutes and Training

Hubbard Diversity ROI Institute

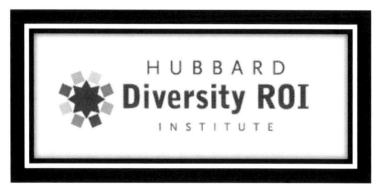

The **Hubbard Diversity ROI Institute** is the leading resource on Diversity ROI Analytics Research, Consulting, Training, and Networking for practitioners of the Hubbard Diversity ROI Methodology (DROI®). The Hubbard Diversity ROI (DROI®) Institute — is an *"applied sciences"* organization dedicated to the development of processes and methods that demonstrate Diversity's measurable value and performance improvement impact on an organization's bottom-line.

Intentional Diversity Transformation

We provide **Diversity ROI Certification Training** (only available from Hubbard & Hubbard, Inc.), analytics research, consulting, benchmarking, publications and online analytical services and tools utilizing the Hubbard Diversity ROI Methodology®.

Earn Six Professional Certifications in Diversity ROI - Available ONLY from Hubbard & Hubbard, Inc.

By enrolling, you can achieve certification as a:
- Certified Diversity Trainer (CDT)
- Certified Diversity Advisor (CDA)
- Certified Diversity Performance Consultant/Technologist (CDPC)
- Certified Diversity Business Partner (CDBP)
- Certified Diversity Strategist (CDS)
- Certified Diversity Intervention Specialist (CDIS)

These Certifications can only be obtained from Hubbard & Hubbard, Inc. You can become Level-I up to Level III Certified in the Hubbard Diversity ROI (DROI®)Methodology

Imagine Your Name:_____, CDA, CDT (with these or other earned credentials after your name)

These certification processes are designed to help you build professional skills, knowledge and confidence to effectively

Intentional Diversity Transformation

improve the performance of your organization with measurable results. For example:

- **Certified Diversity Advisor (CDA)** - Perfect for Diversity Council Members and ERG/BRG Leaders and Members responsible for organizational change and "coaching/advising" the organization through the change process. Participants are taught organizational analysis, coaching and influence skills, ROI Analysis Methods, and more.

- **Certified Diversity Trainer (CDT)** - Perfect for Internal Trainers who want to learn professional Instructional Systems Design (ISD) and Diversity Training Return on Investment (DTROI) Analysis Methods for any Diversity Training Initiative they create and implement.

- **Certified Diversity Performance Consultant / Technologist (CDPC)** - Perfect for those in an "Analyst Role" who need/want the skill set to analyze the Return on Investment impact of any Diversity Initiative they create and implement.

- **Certified Diversity Strategist (CDS)** - Perfect for those in a Diversity Leadership Role who must build Diversity Strategic Plans and Change Implementation Strategies that must demonstrate financial and other performance impacts on the organization's bottom-line.

Intentional Diversity Transformation

- **Certified Diversity Business Partner (CDBP)** Advanced, Senior-level (Level III) Diversity ROI Certification - Perfect for those who need to apply Advanced ROI business and industry knowledge to partner with clients in identifying workplace and business improvement opportunities to leverage differences, similarities and complexities for performance improvement; evaluates possible solutions and recommends solutions that will have a positive impact on performance and business results; gains client agreement and commitment to proposed solutions and collaboratively develops an overall implementation strategy that includes evaluating the ROI impact on business performance; uses appropriate cultural and inclusive interpersonal and coaching styles and other communication methods to build effective long-term relationships with the client; utilizes advanced problem-solving and data analysis and change methods to create measurable differences in the organization's performance.

- etc.

You Receive an Advanced Analysis Toolkit: Each Certification Level will enable you to leave certified to use a comprehensive toolkit of decision-support, diverse work team analysis, change management assessments, performance models, and other tools that are customized for your specific area of expertise.

Intentional Diversity Transformation

Hubbard Diversity Measurement & Productivity Institute

Professional Competency-based Training and Skill-building

Although interest in measuring the effects of diversity has been growing, the topic still challenges even the most sophisticated and progressive diversity departments. Managers know they must begin to show how diversity is linked to the bottom-line or they will have difficulty maintaining funding, gaining support, and assessing progress. The **Hubbard Diversity Measurement & Productivity Institute** (HDM&P) provides on-going, solution-based skill building with a focus on measuring organizational productivity and results.

Intentional Diversity Transformation

Hubbard & Hubbard, Inc. Products and Services

Products Web
www.diversitysuperstore.com

Hubbard ERG and BRG ROI Institute

ERG and BRG Training, Skill-building, and ROI Measurement Techniques for Resource Group Leaders, Sponsors, and Members

http://www.ergandbrgroiinstitute.com/

Join Us! We can help increase your Group's effectiveness and bottom line impact. As a member of the Hubbard ERG and BRG

Intentional Diversity Transformation

ROI Institute, you will acquire expert ROI (Return on Investment) services and ERG and BRG support resources. Our ERG and BRG Institute team of experts will provide critical advice, tools, templates and processes that produce a value-added ROI impact for all of your initiatives.

Let us help you create an entire ERG and BRG strategy and ERG and BRG process from concept to delivery, as we have for many Fortune 500™ and Fortune 100™ companies around the world.

We can help you measure the Return on Investment (ROI) impact of any Employee Resource Group's (ERGs) and Business Resource Group's (BRGs) initiative as well as any other initiatives, goals and strategies.

As a member, you will have access to ERG/BRG focused surveys, member development tools, automated ROI calculators, worksheets, templates, case studies, over 300 formulas, and much, much, more!

Metriclink Dashboard and Scorecard Services

MetricLINK®

Comprehensive Online Performance Measurement and Management Services for Organizational Excellence

Intentional Diversity Transformation

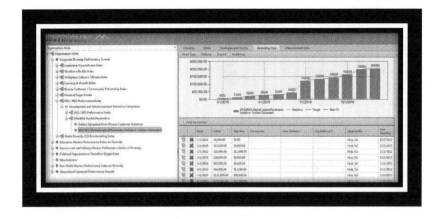

Now you can develop, track, analyze and report your ERG and BRG ROI initiatives using a state-of-the-art online service that was designed with ERGs and BRGs in mind. Practical and easy-to-use, this service gives your group an advanced project planning and Diversity ROI analytics tool to demonstrate your strategic bottom-line impact in data based, financial terms.

Performance Spotlights and Publishing Opportunities

As a member of the Hubbard ERG and BRG Institute, your ERG/BRG efforts can be showcased. Our Performance Spotlights (PS) is a place where Hubbard ERG and BRG Institute members can find ERG/BRG stories of success, learn how a challenge was addressed, or how an ERG/BRG was utilized for performance improvement.

Intentional Diversity Transformation

It is a place where we spotlight and provide you with a strategy, tool, or tip. We can highlight the success of your efforts and enroll your Group's *ROI case study* and work in our **ROI Awards and Recognition Program** and/or **Publish Your Case Study in a Diversity ROI Casebook. If you would like to discuss a potential case study for publication, please contact us.**

Measuring ROI of Diversity Initiatives, ERG/BRG Initiatives, and Other Webinars

We provide members with "tool-based" Webinars on a variety of subjects that are important to your group's growth and development. Check our site at www.hubbardnhubbardinc.com, and/or http://www.ergandbrgroiinstitute.com/ under "Institute Events" for current details and programming. Our goal is to provide you and your group with resources and tools that help you drive measurable ROI-based performance that increases you success!

We can be reached by email message at myrahub@aol.com, edhub@aol.com, or Call: **(707) 481-2268,** we are happy to help.

Index

A

Adoption Evaluation
    definition of, 261
Adoption Rate Success Gate
    definition of, 262
Analytics, 163
    definition of, 163
Assumptions, External Factors, & Contingencies
    Explanation of, 218
ATD
    formerly ASTD, 72

B

balanced scorecard, 3, 25, 49, 132, 203, 204
Basarab, 248
BCR
    calculation, 155
Behavioral Diversity, 144
Belief Evaluation
    definition of, 259
benefit
    Benefits of logic models, 226
Building Centers of Diversity Excellence, 99
Business and Performance Needs Analysis, 40, 44
Business Diversity, 145

C

Calculating the Diversity Return on Investment
    process to, 155
Certifications in Diversity ROI, 282
Challenges of Quantification, 120
combined spending power
    of individual racial groups, 81
Contextual and External Factors, 219
Convert the Contribution to Money, 152
Cost of Not utilizing Diversity and Inclusion, 83
create excellence in performance
    using Diversity, 103
C-Suite, 72

D

Data Isolation, 150
D-BAM, 64, 71, 72
D-BAM with sample D&I strategies, 64
D-BAMs®, 56
Diversity
    as a competitive advantage, 77

definition of, 143
four dimensions of Diversity, 73
Diversity and Inclusion's Value and Worth
   Explanation of, 270
diversity as a strategic asset, 66
Diversity Business Alignment Map, 64
Diversity Business Alignment Maps, 161
Diversity Links to Productivity and Performance, 86
Diversity management
   definition of, 73
Diversity Management
   definition of, 144
diversity measurement
   characteristics of skilled professionals, 105
Diversity Measurement Strategy, 135
Diversity Performance Consultant/Evaluator Certification, 255
diversity return-on-investment, 138, 143, 145, 147, 149, 152, 155, 158
Diversity ROI, 281, 282, 284, 288, 289
Diversity ROI (DROI®), 281
Diversity ROI Analytics, 281
Diversity Scorecard, 69, 235
Diversity Transformational Analytics®, 4, 6, 8, 41, 47, 158, 178, 207
Diversity's Contribution
   business contributions of, 96
diversity-maturity
   characteristics of, 100

Dr. R. Roosevelt Thomas, 13, 27, 73, 100
DROI Certification Workshops, 221
   Link to attend, 221
DROI%
   process to calculate, 155
DROI®, 5, 37, 38, 39, 47, 106, 141, 159, 244, 274, 275, 276

E

Edward E. Hubbard, 68, 69
Effect
   definition of, 133
   Examples of assumptions, 218

H

How to Calculate Diversity Return on Investment, 26, 161
Hubbard Diversity Business Alignment Maps, 56
Hubbard Diversity Measurement & Productivity Institute, 285
Hubbard Diversity Measurement and Productivity (HDM&P) Institute, 38, 70
Hubbard Diversity Measurement Sciences, 177
Hubbard Diversity Performance Drivers Model®, 31, 32
Hubbard Diversity Return on Investment Institute, 31
Hubbard Diversity ROI Analysis Model, 145, 146
Hubbard Diversity ROI Institute, 281

Intentional Diversity Transformation

I

Identifying Intangible Benefits, 156
Impact Evaluation
    definition of, 265
impact of diversity on the bottom line
    examples of, 92
Initiative Identification
    definition of, 240
Intended Transformational Impacts
    definition of, 4, 162, 163, 177, 202
Intention Evaluation
    definition of, 254
Intention Score
    definition of, 255
Intention Success Gate
    definition of, 254
Isolate Diversity's Contribution, 150

J

Judith Rosner, 68

K

Kaplan and Norton, 3, 25, 27, 204

L

Lawrence Bayos, 75
Links between Diversity and R&D cycle time, 137
logic model
    When to apply them, 222
Logic Model, 4, 5, 8, 158, 163, 166, 167, 168, 169, 170, 171, 172, 174, 176, 177, 178, 202, 207, 216
Logic Model categories and metrics
    Sample Metrics, 178
Logic Models
    examples of, 12, 164, 177, 184, 224

M

Marilyn Loden, 68
Measuring Diversity Results, 26, 37, 58, 69, 109, 235, 244
Metriclink, 46, 47, 48, 51
Metriclink Dashboard and Scorecard Services, 287

N

Needs Analysis, 209, 263

O

Organizational Transformation and Change, 183
Origins of Transformational and Transactional Dynamics, 186
    Definition of, 186
Outcome Measures, 132
Outcomes
    Types of, 213

P

Predictive Analytics for Diversity (PAD[tm]) Sequence

Step for Implementing, 273
*Predictive Analytics for Diversity*tm,
    247, 248, 249, 250, 253
Predictive Evaluation, 6, 244, 274, 276
Productivity, 90

R

R. Roosevelt Thomas, 68
Retention, 87

S

Service-Profit Chain, 58, 86, 109, 126
strategic business partner, 61, 70, 73
strategic business partners, 107
Strategic Impact
    Examples of, 215
Strategic Initiative Plan Alignment Components
    definition of, 241
superficial strategy map, 123

T

The Diversity Scorecard, 11, 201, 202, 203, 206
The Diversity Scorecard: Evaluating the Impact of Diversity on Organizational Performance, 11
Track and Assess Progress, 158
Tracking/Reporting, 157
Traditional input-output model, 133
TRANSACTIONAL Factors
    Model of, 190
TRANSFORMATIONAL Factors, 187
typically define their diversity
    Typical definition of Diversity, 63

W

Webinars, 289
Workforce Diversity, 144